Meeting the Needs of Gifted and Talented Students

C000009829

Also available in the Meeting the Needs series:
Meeting the Needs of Students with Dyslexia – June Massey

Also available from Network Continuum:
Pocket PAL: Successful Provision for Able and Talented Children – Barry Teare
Challenging Resources for Able and Talented Children – Barry Teare
Effective Provision for Able and Talented Children – Barry Teare
Effective Resources for Able and Talented Children – Barry Teare
More Effective Resources for Able and Talented Children – Barry Teare
Enrichment Activities for Able and Talented Children – Barry Teare
Problem-solving and Thinking Skills Resources for Able and Talented Children – Barry Teare
Help Your Talented Child – Barry Teare

Available from Continuum:
Able, Gifted and Talented – Janet Bates and Sarah Munday

Meeting the Needs of Gifted and Talented Students

Gwen Goodhew

network
continuum

Continuum International Publishing Group
Network Continuum
The Tower Building
11 York Road
London, SE1 7NX

80 Maiden Lane, Suite 704
New York, NY 10038

www.networkcontinuum.co.uk
www.continuumbooks.com

© Gwen Goodhew 2009

All rights reserved. No part of this publication may be reproduced or transmitted in any form or by any means, electronic or mechanical, including photocopying, recording, or any information storage or retrieval system, without prior permission in writing from the publishers.

Gwen Goodhew has asserted her right under the Copyright, Designs and Patents Act, 1988, to be identified as Author of this work.

British Library Cataloguing-in-Publication Data
A catalogue record for this book is available from the British Library.

ISBN: 9781855394650 (paperback)

Library of Congress Cataloguing-in-Publication Data
A catalog record of this book is availble from the Library of Congress.

Typeset by YHT Ltd, London
Printed and bound in Great Britain by Ashford Colour Press Ltd, Gosport, Hampshire

Contents

Acknowledgements

My sincere thanks go to all the individuals and groups who have helped me with the writing of this book, but especially to the Benson and Wellman families; John Stanfield; Ellie Shiell; Liz Ponting; the Bay Tree Centre, Brixton; Johanna Raffau and NACE; Joseph Renzulli; the Department for Schools, Children and Families (dscf) for allowing me to use some of their materials; the Sutton Trust; Carol Archer and the teachers of Warrington and Cheshire; Carol Cummings and Aileen Hoare of Day a Week School (DWS) and the children of the Bunbury DWS; Malasree Home; Department of Engineering, Liverpool University; and my husband, Peter, for stepping in whenever my ICT skills failed me.

Acknowledgements

Introduction

Although able or gifted and talented education has a much higher profile in the United Kingdom than it did ten or 15 years ago, it is still a bit of a Cinderella in the education world. Yet the need for appropriate provision for our most able students could hardly be more pressing. At a national level and, indeed, throughout the developed world, there is a growing demand for a highly educated, adaptable and creative workforce and very little demand for unskilled workers. We do not need robots but people to design the robots. There is real concern that so many of our potential high-flyers are underachieving, lacking both confidence and aspiration, that universities, research organizations and big companies are increasingly turning to motivated foreign youth to fill the gaps. If as a nation we are to remain competitive in the face of challenge from the new economies of India and China, we must tackle this culture of underachievement.

Tackling underachievement is just as important at the personal level. Learning experiences that inspire, challenge and motivate our school students, whether they are 4 or 19, could help to stem what Lampl (2007) referred to as 'a sickening waste of talent' – a waste that can produce a general dissatisfaction, inhibiting ambition and even damaging personal relationships and mental health. Sadly, the differences in life opportunities between the middle classes and the poor are growing in this country, not decreasing as one might expect. The reasons are complex but the outcome is that a cycle of underachievement is perpetuated from one generation to another. Opportunities for self-improvement and escape are perceived to be fewer. In such a climate it is all too easy for talent that is not suitably channelled to be misdirected into anti-social behaviour or crime.

It follows then that if we are to avoid the problems that underachievement creates at both societal and personal levels, each school should first identify a pool of potential talent/giftedness, then nurture the policy makers and creative stars of tomorrow through exciting, personalized education programmes. This is not easy but there is abundant evidence to show that where schools make effective provision for their most able students, standards are raised generally throughout a school. Everyone benefits, not just an elite.

Despite concerns about underachievement and the low priority often afforded to gifted and talented education, a number of recent government initiatives in the UK have created an excited buzz within gifted and talented education circles and should help to force it to the top of the education agenda. These include:

- a gifted and talented element being incorporated into the National Strategies with leading teachers for gifted and talented education being identified and trained in all schools
- the development and promotion of National Quality Standards in Gifted and Talented Education by the dcsf
- the drawing together of services for children through the *Every Child Matters* white paper with its focus on improving access to education for some disadvantaged groups
- the setting up of a national register for gifted and talented students
- the establishment of regional Excellence Hubs to provide local high quality opportunities for these students
- extended school days through which it is hoped to offer exciting and different learning experiences.

It remains to be seen whether the high expectations engendered by these initiatives will be fulfilled, but these are nonetheless exciting times for gifted and talented education.

This book is a resource for all teachers and teaching assistants in all key stages, who are working to improve provision for their most able students. School governors, especially any whose brief covers gifted and talented education, should also find it useful in helping them to gain a better understanding of gifted and talented education.

Meeting the Needs of Gifted and Talented Students will cover the main issues of:

- terminology
- identification
- school structures to support the most able
- general classroom provision
- gifted and talented pupils with additional needs.

Although *Meeting the Needs of Gifted and Talented Students* is targeted primarily at the UK market, much of the material could be relevant to educators in other countries.

What do we mean by Gifted, Talented and Exceptionally Able?

1

Different Perceptions of Giftedness

In the Introduction, the importance of identifying and nurturing high ability or potential was stressed but, before exploring how this can be done, an understanding of the words able, gifted, talented and exceptionally able, as they are being used throughout this book, needs to be established.

It is always interesting, during professional development sessions, to ask groups of teachers to jot down their definitions of gifted or giftedness and post them round the room. The discussion that follows is invariably lively and often heated because the exercise reveals the wide range of responses and emotions the words provoke.

For some, the word gifted applies only to the giants of our civilizations – Mozart, Michelangelo, Einstein et al. – in fact, such rarities that these teachers do not expect to meet a truly gifted student in their lifetime and work on the assumption that it is a problem they will never have to deal with in the classroom. It can be difficult for teachers with this idea about giftedness to engage with discussion about classroom provision for gifted students, especially if they are working in a deprived area.

For others, especially teachers whose ideas have been moulded during the grammar school selection era, the issue is quite straightforward – a gifted student is defined by his/her score on an IQ test – a score of 130+ (depending on the test) means that a student is gifted, a score of 129 means that he is not. This is a very comfortable definition to work with because it is simple and it is easy to identify the students who qualify. The downside is that many students of extraordinary ability are overlooked when such an approach is used because IQ tests measure such a limited range of abilities.

The ideas of Joseph Renzulli have permeated many schools throughout the UK, USA and Australia and these ideas are reflected in the definitions of giftedness other teachers write down. Renzulli believes that many children of *above average ability* (not necessarily exceptional ability) are capable of displaying giftedness if they also have *commitment* to a task combined with *creativity* – the ability to bring something new to the task. This has become known as his Three-Ringed Conception of Gift-edness. Renzulli (1998) believes that a child's general level of ability is more or less fixed but that creativity and commitment are more dependent on the opportunities and stimuli provided. There might be long periods of inactivity but when real engagement takes place, gifted performance is possible – hence the importance of appropriate provision, a large talent pool in which to look for potential giftedness and exciting teachers who inspire students to become engaged in this way. This concept of giftedness or potential giftedness embraces a much larger proportion of the school population than the one dependent on a high IQ score. Renzulli suggests that a talent pool of 15–20 per cent of the school population should be considered when looking for gifted potential.

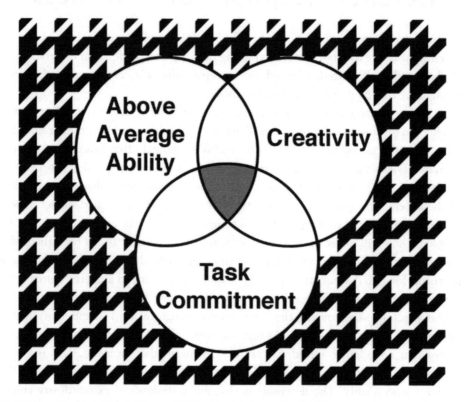

The Three-Ringed Conception of Giftedness – Renzulli (1998)

There are teachers who use the words able, gifted and talented interchangeably for all areas and levels of endeavour and achievement, while others use the words able, talented and gifted as the top three rungs of a hierarchy of ability; for example, an able musician probably plays in the school orchestra, a talented musician is technically very competent and plays for the county youth orchestra but a gifted musician, whether a conductor, trombonist or composer, is both technically very competent and has the ability to bring something new and exciting to interpretation or composition. Again, as with Renzulli's ideas, the concept of giftedness is linked with creativity – the ability to generate lots of ideas (fluency), look at a problem from an unusual viewpoint (flexibility), develop an idea (elaboration) and come up with something new (originality).

In many education circles, giftedness and talent are defined in terms of the amount of additional resources students need. If a child's learning needs cannot easily be met in the ordinary classroom with his or her peers because s/he is achieving at a level comparable with students a few years older, s/he may be considered gifted or talented. Several US states use definitions of giftedness that include this idea of high ability combined with a need for additional resource. North Dakota for example, decided that: '"A student who is gifted" means an individual who is identified by qualified professionals as being capable of high performance and who needs educational programs and services beyond those normally provided in a regular education program.' (Davidson Institute GT-Cybersource 2007)

At the other end of the spectrum from those who regard giftedness as a rarity are teachers who believe that everyone has a gift or talent and that the real challenge is to find it. Without doubt, there is a huge waste of talent but whether the overuse of the words gifted and talented is helpful is another matter.

Not only do teachers' ideas of giftedness vary but so do their attitudes to it. Whatever its exact meaning, giftedness is not always regarded as a positive attribute. The egalitarianism of the mid-twentieth century and the move away from academic selection left the UK teaching profession a legacy of suspicion towards anything that could be regarded as elitist. It was in this climate of ambivalence to giftedness that NACE, the National Association for Able Children in Education, was set up in the UK in the 1980s. Teachers knew that gifted children were being short-changed but using the word 'able' was more acceptable to some colleagues and less likely to provoke hostility. There are still schools, especially in socially deprived areas, where there is a reluctance to admit that the most able children need special provision because giftedness is associated with pushy middle-class parents trying to get more than their share of the education cake.

The English Gifted and Talented Programme

The last ten years have seen some interesting developments in gifted education in England. In an attempt to raise teachers' expectations of pupils in inner city schools, the programme Excellence in Cities was put in place in 1997. Gifted and talented education was one of the strands of this project. Schools were given very clear guidelines on who should be part of this programme:

- the gifted were those with high ability or potential in academic subjects
- talented pupils were to be those with outstanding ability or potential in sport, PE, art and design, music or the performing arts
- regardless of the general level of ability within the school, teachers were to identify 5–10 per cent as gifted and talented
- no more than a third of these children were to be talented
- the gifted and talented cohort was to be representative of the school's social and ethnic mix.

This was quite a tall order and one that challenged many teachers' understanding of giftedness. Not surprisingly there was some resistance to this approach for a number of reasons:

1. There was no consistency in the gifted and talented cohort across schools. As part of this programme, secondary schools were expected to work in clusters to provide additional support for these students. This could be very difficult when selective schools were involved. Their gifted and talented cohorts were very different from those in non-selective schools that had a disproportionately small number of academically able students. Some pupils became embarrassed by, and defensive about, what they perceived as their lack of ability in comparison with others.

2. A gifted or talented child in what might be termed a 'sink' school could end up in the lower sets if he were to transfer across a city to a more successful or selective school. Teachers asked if it was fair to put gifted or talented tags metaphorically round the necks of children who would find that they were not judged to be such in the wider world.

3. Schools found it very difficult to make sure that the gifted and talented cohort was representative of a school's social and ethnic mix. In schools with large numbers of migrants and a rapidly changing population, it was difficult to identify those who would fit into the programme.

4. Teachers were reluctant to exclude from the programme pupils whose work and attitude were good, to make way for those who were less motivated but were perceived to have potential. They wanted to use the programme as encouragement for hard work and compliance.

5. The definitions of giftedness and talent given to schools did not match those of the National Academy for Gifted and Talented Youth, which was established at the same time (since superseded by YGT – Young, Gifted and Talented). It was providing for the national gifted cohort – those in the top 5 per cent of the national ability pool – a very different group of pupils from many schools' gifted and talented cohorts. This meant that students could be described as gifted within their schools but were not sufficiently gifted to be part of the national programme.

To overcome the problems associated with this use of the words 'gifted and talented', many schools elected to use the word 'able' to describe their top 5–10 per cent of the ability range and to use 'exceptionally able' to describe those who would fit into the top 5 per cent at national level.

The Excellence in Cities project has come to an end. Even though the definitions of gifted and talented caused some difficulties, there were advantages in scrutinizing a larger talent pool than had been the practice and of having a more flexible view of gifted and talented behaviours. Children who had been overlooked in the past, especially where expectations of young people from particular ethnic or social groups had been low, benefited from the broader identification criteria adopted. As a result of these observations, a national gifted and talented programme has been put in place in England in which the definitions of giftedness and talent as used in Excellence in Cities have been only slightly modified.

The word 'gifted' describes 'students who have the ability to excel academically in one or more subject such as English, drama or technology'. The word 'talented' describes 'students who have the ability to excel in practical skills, such as sport, leadership, artistic performance'. (DfES 2007:17) There is an assumption that all schools should be looking to identify about 10 per cent of their pupils as gifted or talented.

In more recent documentation, the government has also identified another group they call 'the exceptionally able' which they define as 'Learners who demonstrate or have the potential to demonstrate extremely high levels of ability compared to their peers across the entire population . . . A quantitative measure which can be used as an indicator is the top 2% nationally for one or more academic and talent areas.' (Department for Children, Schools and Families 2008:4)

The big difference to note between gifted and talented and exceptionally able is that the abilities of gifted and talented pupils are being judged against the performance of others within their schools whereas the performance of the exceptionally able is being seen in a national context.

Terminology in this Book

Even though the terminology above, especially in respect of the word gifted, is significantly different from that used in many parts of North America and Australia, it seems sensible to use the language that all leading teachers of gifted and talented education in England will be exposed to.

The *gifted* will be those pupils whose performance or potential in academic subjects such as English, drama, foreign languages, mathematics, the humanities, design technology or science, is significantly ahead of their peers and would place them, very roughly, in the top 10 per cent of a school's ability range. It is important to emphasize that pupils who are showing the potential to operate at this level, even if at this stage there are factors that stop them achieving, should be included. Students who are both gifted and have an additional need, such as dyslexia or a behavioural problem, should also be included.

The *talented* will be those with marked ability in art and design, music, sport, physical education or performing arts, such that they are achieving at considerably beyond the level expected of that age group within a school. Their performance or potential marks them out from their peers. Another group of pupils who will be considered as talented are those with outstanding leadership abilities and/or interpersonal skills. Students who lead successful groups of young entrepreneurs would fall into this group, as would those who shine in roles such as head boy/girl, head of house and organizers of class or school events. Neither should we overlook those with such well-developed social skills that they are able to defuse difficult situations or befriend solitary students.

There are some subjects that may fit into both the gifted and talented categories. In drama, for example, you could argue that the brilliant young actor who brings an original interpretation to a very demanding role is both talented because of the practical skills involved and gifted because of the intellectual demands of the task. The same is true of music. A young musician who produces an outstanding and highly original composition is certainly talented but is he also displaying gifted behaviour because of the academic skills required? There is no right or wrong answer, but it is something that teachers will continue to debate. In the same way there are, of course, many people who are naturally both gifted and talented in very different fields. Winston Churchill was a leader, writer, historian and artist; Albert Einstein played the violin; Menzies Campbell, the former leader of the Liberal Democrats, was an international athlete as well as a lawyer and politician; Carol Vorderman is a mathematician and showbiz personality; Condoleezza Rice is an eminent political scientist and was a music prodigy. To some extent the lines drawn between gifts and talents are artificial but as long as teachers, parents and students understand the terminology and students falling into both groups are given appropriate support and status, this is not important.

The *exceptionally able* will be those whose performance or potential is *extremely high* in relation to their peers throughout the country. It might be useful to think of them as representing the top 2 per cent of the ability range but it is important not to get hung up on percentages. It is these students who are most likely to require *very* different provision if their needs are to be met.

For convenience and simplicity, the word *able* will often be used in this book as a general 'cover all' to include the gifted, talented and exceptionally able.

Gifted and Talented Cohorts should not be Fixed

One important point to make is this: a school's gifted and talented cohort is not expected to be fixed and should change over time. The reasoning is that gifts and talents may emerge at any stage during students' schooling (and beyond). Some students who start well may begin to plateau and make less progress while others, after a slower beginning, start to surge ahead. Distressingly, recent research funded by the Sutton Trust, has found that bright 3-year-olds from working class backgrounds are already losing ground to their middle-class peers by the time they are five and their progress slows further as they get older. It is to be hoped that if schools get their identification strategies right, this loss of potential will be avoided. However, the fact remains that the fluidity of the gifted and talented cohort in schools will need very careful handling. Teachers are not accustomed to giving 'gifted' tags and then taking them away. There is a tradition of applying the terms gifted or talented for life. Moving students out of the gifted and talented cohort is undertaken with understandable reluctance because it is likely to discourage them, but if teachers are not prepared to do this, then late developers will not be given the opportunities they deserve. This is a dilemma that schools will have to face.

Whatever the concerns about the current use of the words gifted and talented, both in this book and beyond, there can be little doubt that a strategy that casts a wider net in order to recognize and nurture able students who have been overlooked in the past is preferable to a more exclusive approach.

2 Identifying Gifted and Talented Students

Why do we need to Identify the Gifted and Talented?

Identifying potentially gifted and talented students has never been an exact science, and never will be, but that does not mean that we should not try to do the job as well as possible. Returning again to the recent report from the Sutton Trust (2007) on *Recent Changes in Intergenerational Mobility* there is clear evidence that we are allowing potentially gifted and talented students from poorer socio-economic backgrounds to slip slowly out of the picture as their sometimes less able but more affluent peers pass them by. Obviously we want children from middle-class backgrounds to be high achievers too, but we do need to find ways of nurturing those whose parents do not have the resources or know-how to foster their abilities.

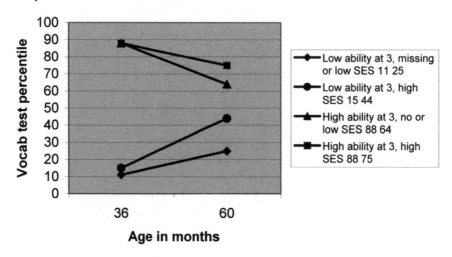

Evolution of Test Scores by Early Ability and Socio-Economic Status in Millennium Cohort Study

This figure shows clearly that one of the purposes of identifying high potential must be to tackle underachievement. But there are other important reasons. When we know which students are or might be able in a particular field, it allows us to:

- match provision to the learner
- motivate students and create a more rewarding learning environment
- raise standards. There is ample evidence from Ofsted reports that schools that identify and provide for their most able students provide a good education for all.

Myths about Gifted and Talented Students

Before we can begin to explore some possible identification strategies, a few myths regarding our most able students need to be dispelled.

Myth 1: If they've got it, they'll make it. Cream always rises to the top.

The only response to this is, 'If only!' We simply have to look at the previous figure, knowing that the trends identified there continue throughout students' schooling, to see that this is not the case. There are many tales of gifted dyslexics succeeding against the odds, but the vast majority had supportive and knowledgeable home backgrounds and, in several cases, exclusive fee-paying schools or private tutors. People like Richard Branson and Winston Churchill fall into this category. They did not get to the top unaided.

Myth 2: All gifted and talented children are recognizable from a very early age, so catch them young and the job is done.

There is some truth in the idea that mathematical ability and musical ability tend to appear quite early, given the right circumstances, and that children who read early *may* go on to do well in academic subjects, but there are other gifts that demand life experiences before they can flourish. Potential playwrights, historians, philosophers, entrepreneurs and economists may not begin to show their abilities until the later stages of schooling. Other students do not show their abilities in the early years because of emotional immaturity or limited pre-school learning experiences.

Myth 3: They always do well in standardized tests.

Again this is untrue because standardized tests, such as IQ tests and Cognitive Abilities Tests (CATs), measure a relatively narrow band of abilities. Children from immigrant communities may not have the cultural or linguistic background to show their capabilities. A few of our most exceptional students either become bored by the tests and do not give them their full attention or are confused because they can spot alternative answers that the test devisers had not appreciated. Below is an example that is often used.

Underline the odd one out

Root

Trunk

Hare

Leaf

Bough

Obviously the expected response is 'hare' but the child who underlines 'trunk' because all the others have homophones – route, hair, lief, bow – will get no marks even though his/her reasoning is spot on and the vocabulary remarkable.

Case Study

In one comprehensive school that used Cognitive Abilities Tests (CATs) as a guide to setting new entrants, a young man of truly exceptional ability was rescued from a sojourn in the lower sets by a teacher who knew his family well. She asked the head of Year 7 to look at his paper again, after seeing the proposed setting arrangements. The head of year reported that his test paper was incomplete and covered in chess moves. Further investigations revealed that he had not endeared himself to his last primary school teacher, a stickler for accurate spelling and neat handwriting, because he did not hand in homework and day-dreamed through lessons. So her reference to the comprehensive school had been luke-warm at best. His parents supervised his homework, but often found it later either in the bin or screwed up under the settee. When challenged he explained that there was no point handing it in because the teacher would still find fault and he could not write neatly. The boy was already playing chess at a very high level and peers reported that, although they liked him very much, they never understood what he was talking about because his ideas were 'off the wall'. The Year 7 head interviewed the boy and on that basis placed him in the top sets. He continued to exasperate his teachers but his ability was recognized and nur-tured. He left the school to study PPE at Oxford.

Myth 4: The gifted are good at most subjects.

Again this is not the case. There are, of course, good all-rounders but there are many gifted or talented students who excel in only one or two areas of the curriculum or in a group of closely related subjects such as maths and science, sport and PE or the humanities. Having a real interest in a particular field is often the key to high potential or performance.

Gifted and Talented Students who may be Overlooked

From the very earliest days of schooling there have been some children for whom expectations are not sufficiently high. We can hope that initiatives like Sure Start in England and new foundation assessments for children moving from nursery and reception to Key Stage 1 will overcome some of these problems. Unfortunately, the most needy children are the most difficult to draw into pre-school provision and there is every likelihood that their abilities will continue to be underestimated.

Expectations for Different Groups of Children

Higher expectations	Lower expectations
Attractive	Unprepossessing
Confident	Shy
Neat and well organized	Disorganized with poor motor skills
Middle-class	Poor
Supportive home	Large family with low-attaining older siblings
Birthday in first half of school year	Summer birthday and male
Female	Male
White, Chinese and Indian	Some other ethnic groups
Very verbal	Poor verbal skills
Well-behaved	Disruptive
Socially adept	Immature

Most of the items in the table above are self-explanatory but it is worth looking at the summer birthday issue in more detail. A class of reception children in September will have some children who are only just 4 and others almost a year older. These will have had a quarter more life and learning experiences than the younger children! There is a tendency to underestimate how much very young children do compare themselves with others and they can become disheartened at the very earliest stages of schooling if others appear to cope more easily than they do. Reception teachers are sensitive to these age differences, but teachers become less sensitive as children move up through the school and the feeling of inadequacy can remain and grow. Even when students are in their teens, a year can make a big difference to their maturity. Boys seem to find the early disadvantage of being young in a school year particularly difficult to overcome. It is always a good idea for 'young in year' pupils to be drawn to the attention of classroom teachers, especially where underachievement is suspected.

At all stages of schooling, identification strategies need to have the following in common:

1. They should be ongoing. The job of identification is never done and indicators of potential should be recorded and acted on quickly. Updating once a year is not sufficient.
2. They should be wide-ranging so that all kinds of abilities are identified; the data gathered should be presented as a profile. Single scores should be avoided.
3. They should be coordinated across the school so that all teachers are aware of a child's potential. The information should be passed to (and used by!) receiving schools.
4. Parents and outside agencies, such as sports clubs, performing arts groups and music schools, should be involved in the identification process. Students, too, should be offered opportunities to talk about their interests and strengths.
5. The register of gifted and talented students held by each school should be scrutinized to make sure that different ethnic and social groups are fairly represented and that potentially gifted or talented children with additional needs are not overlooked. Care should also be taken to avoid stereotyping.
6. They should be used to inform personalization of the curriculum, not simply compiled and ignored.
7. They should be fair and transparent.

Provision as an Identification Strategy

When a list of identification strategies is given, it is quite usual to see the word 'provision' tacked on at the end. Yet what happens in the classroom and in extra-curricular activities should be the centrepiece of any school identification policy. When students experience something that grips their attention or motivates them to find out more or amuses and entertains them, the potential for high performance becomes apparent. The approach known as PIP – Provide, Identify, Provide – is a good starting point, but if teaching methods and delivery are always the same, then the same children will be identified over and over again – hence the addition of 'Provide Something Different' into the cycle is very important.

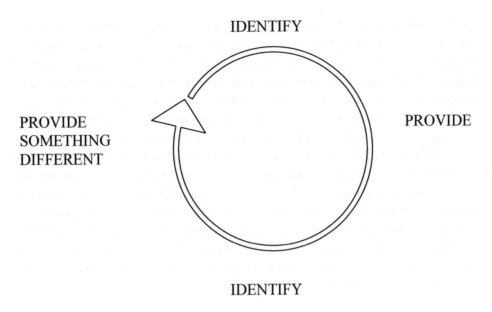

IDENTIFY

PROVIDE

PROVIDE
SOMETHING
DIFFERENT

IDENTIFY

Cyclical Provision and Identification

Case Study

> The same teacher had taught French to a class of Year 10 pupils for two years. She was very competent and well organized but all her lessons followed the same pattern – working through the next section of the textbook, question and answer round the class, writing out relevant verbs and setting a short task for homework. A small group of girls, who enjoyed the security of this approach, flourished but the rest of the class, especially the boys, were bored and resentful. When this teacher left, another took over whose approach was totally different. She taught the class jokes in French and invited students to contribute their own acceptable jokes in the language. She brought in sets of nursery rhymes and stories for young children in French and soon had the class reading them together before acting them out and setting some to music. One group of boys created a play with music out of one of the stories and went to the local nursery school to perform it. It was a huge success. The teacher was mindful that this approach would not suit all pupils and that there were occasions when academic rigour was needed. So she returned to whiteboard and talk or the textbook and more structured activities at regular intervals. At the end of Year 11 several pupils, who had not shown any interest in French earlier in their secondary school careers, went on to gain As and A*s at GCSE with some opting to study it at AS level.

The Sports Approach

Freeman (1998:18) advocates another form of identification by provision, which she calls The Sports Approach. Her argument is, that just as with football and other sports where students elect to spend their time practising and playing in teams, if opportunities were provided in a wide range of other activities such as science and modern foreign languages and some guidance were offered, potentially gifted and talented students would be quite capable of selecting activities appropriate to their abilities. Teachers should not need to pre-select. There is much to recommend in this approach as many students complain of being overlooked or rejected for activities that they desperately want to take part in and in which they might, indeed, excel. However, the down side of such an approach is that many able students from poorer homes do not always have the confidence to put themselves forward and there is the usual danger that these opportunities would be taken up entirely by middle-class students unless there was some teacher intervention. There are regular reports from regional groups arranging activities for gifted and talented students that middle-class parents drive their children many miles to make sure they take advantage of anything on offer. Even when these activities are intentionally placed in deprived areas, it is still difficult to involve local students.

Dynamic Assessment

Morley et al. suggest another approach to provision-based identification called Dynamic Assessment. The process could be called assess-intervene-assess in that students' abilities in a particular field are assessed, a teaching programme put in place and then a second assessment takes place. 'The virtue of approaches like this is that they can offer insight into an individual's 'learnability', the ability to take on and use new skills and understanding, which seems to be a good indicator of potential talent.' (Morley et al. 2006:48–9)

Although these comments were made in relation to the teaching of PE and sports, it is easy to see how the same approach could be used in any subject and could be particularly helpful where teachers do not know a group of children well. For example, a mathematics teacher may want to introduce a new topic to a Year 7 group. Having carried out an initial assessment and modified the teaching programme on the basis of the information received from that assessment, a post-provision test would highlight those pupils whose mastery had moved forward markedly, no matter what their starting point, and could indicate high potential in that area.

Dynamic Assessment is most successful where the teacher has a clear idea of the skills or abilities s/he is trying to draw out. If when setting a writing task, a teacher knows that s/he is looking for a student's ability to draw inferences from the information provided, his/her assessment will be based on that and not, as happens so often, on neatness, good spelling, grammar and punctuation and a ready smile.

High Potential and Play

Classroom activities that encourage children to play with words, shapes, materials and ideas will often highlight high ability. In the example below, the teacher was talking about and reading examples of counting poems. Children were then asked to make one of their own, where each number has an animal starting with the same letter and some describing words. Catriona could not spell all the words she wanted to use but she proved to have an astonishing vocabulary!

> Sssssssssssssssssssssssss
> Seven slithering, slimy, scaly, scaring, staring, startling snakes
> Eight enormous, elegant, egg-shaped, erased, ebullient elephants
> Nine nocturnal, naked, noseless, gnu-made, narrow gnomes
> Ten terrifying, toothless, tardy, toy, tin-made, tangerine-coloured, two-year-old, tiny, timid tarantulas
> Catriona (aged 6)

Identification at Key Stage 1 (ages 5–7)

At Key Stage 1 it can be very difficult to make accurate assessments of children's potential. Some will have had a rich and exciting range of learning experiences in the home and in nursery. They may have travelled widely and met people from other cultures. They may have bedrooms full of books and a computer. Others will have had no pre-school education and, in some cases, will have spent most of their lives in homes with a single carer, few books and limited conversation. Most children will have been taught independence skills such as toilet training, using cutlery to feed themselves, dressing and undressing and socializing with adults and peers before they enter schools, others will have to learn these before moving on to other knowledge and skills. There will be children who have had the advantages of a nurturing home but are still physically and emotionally immature. It will take time for these early disadvantages to be overcome and, unfortunately, in some cases, they never will be unless intervention strategies are used. Nonetheless, some evening out should take place over time and late starters may begin to make up ground.

Foundation Stage Profile

One of the best resources for KS1 teachers will be the Foundation Stage Profile, compiled by early years teachers throughout nursery school and reception. For best use to be made of this resource it will be important to make sure that all the different aspects of a child's development are taken into account. When assessing potential, there is a danger that high priority will be given to a child's attainment levels in 'Communication, Language and Literacy' and 'Mathematical Development' and that high achievement in other sections, particularly 'Creativity', will be overlooked.

Crocodile by Ellie, age 4 – The observation skills and creativity displayed by this 4-year-old in her drawings should be taken into account when assessing potential

If this proves to be the case, the seeds of underachievement could be sown for many children. On the other hand, if good use is made of this resource it should help teachers to identify high potential in a wide range of fields and to plan programmes of work that move a child on where attainment is high, while at the same time offering support in weaker areas of the curriculum.

Early Years Able Learners: Identification and Provision

For children between the ages of 4 and 7 years another useful screening device has been produced by the National Association for Able Children in Education (NACE) based on the Nebraska Starry Night Profile. Griffin et al. (1995:34) but with additional supporting materials. It could be used:

- to supplement the Foundation Stage Profile
- where a child enters a school late and there is limited information from previous schools

- for EAL children
- for children with disabilities who are difficult to assess.

Its strength is that it concentrates on behaviours and approaches to learning rather than on achievement and helps teachers to tailor teaching to children's learning styles. It is simple to use; teachers observe children over a period of three weeks and record when a child demonstrates a particular behaviour on a regular basis. Depending on the behaviours shown, the children are likely to fall into one of four dispositions:

- the curious, exploring, moving and doing child
- the verbal, knowing and independent child
- the engaging, centre-stage, socially interactive child
- the quiet, focused, unexpectedly humorous child.

By focusing on these behaviours rather than on achievement, teachers are better able to draw out children's abilities and make appropriate provision.

Creativity Tests

There are some practitioners who advocate the use of creativity tests to identify students with creative potential – those able to think in a different way and to do or make something unusual and unexpected – the very people our society needs. Perhaps the best known of such tests are the ones devised by Paul Torrance (1980) and the Klaus K.Urban and Hans R. Jellen Test for Creative Thinking-Drawing Production TCP-DP (1996). The latter can be used with school students of all ages and involves their completing a picture which, at the initial stage, consists of fragments of figures. Each of the two tests takes 15 minutes and 14 evaluation criteria are provided to help teachers to assess the outcomes. Children enjoy these activities but many teachers would argue that they are able to assess children's creative potential from the broad range of activities they provide in the classroom. It is also the case that creativity is specific to such a narrow field in some students that these tests may not pick them up.

Parents

At this stage of development and later, parents can provide valuable information about children's interests and activities. Children at KS1 can be so disorientated by the school experience that they wander around aimlessly or flit frantically from one activity to another and present as totally different children from those that parents

Diagram 5
Categorization Grid Sheet

National Association
for Able Children
in Education

Name of Child:

Vocabulary
Fluent, detailed, comprehends, uses complex words and sentences, uses facial expression & body language to communicate

Curious
Always asking questions, notices, examines, observes, has insight

Stays Focused
Can be intensely focused if there is sufficient challenge

Acts as an Expert
Sought out by others, seen as a resource, shows how, is responsive, admired

Imaginative
Invents, imitates, pretends, responds to novel stimuli, may have unusual possibly 'silly' ideas

Explores
Experiments, builds, designs, constructs, organises, plays, enjoys learning in unusual ways

Independent
Works alone, initiates, perfectionist, self- critical

Sees the Big Picture
Sees beyond the obvious, recognises pattern, associates, predicts, analyses, theorises

Creative
Shows signs of originality

Visual and Spatial
Advanced spatial awareness, aware of body space, sees in pictures, creates unusual patterns, good at puzzles

Sensitive
Expressive, has insight, thoughtful, helpful, sympathetic, emphatic, anxious, self aware, aware of being different

Mover and Doer
Advanced early motor development, demonstrates, constructs, non-verbal expressive

Problem Solver
Comprehends, reasons, connects, finds, applies past learning, explains, calculates, understands processes

Observant
Notices detail ,quick & accurate recall, alert

Humorous
Original, spontaneous, quick witted, enjoys adult humour, makes jokes

Is Hungry for Attention
Eager to be involved, attempts to be centre stage

A Leader
Initiates, directs, leads, attracts, shows how, offers or extends instructions, helps, advises, encourages

Significant Moments
Unexpected, extraordinary, extra special, difficult to classify, non-conformist

Photocopy this diagram as required

© National Association for Able Children in Education - September 2006

NACE Early Years Able Learners: Indentification & Provision

Diagram 6
Learning Dispositions

National Association
for Able Children
in Education

Disposition 1

These children have a wide general knowledge, ask frequent questions, and are willing to
share and volunteer information to others. Girls are more likely to display their knowledge
through reading and writing whereas boys will be more verbal. Knowledge can be expressed
through reading, writing and speaking, often with good vocabulary. These children are happy to
work in a group or alone, although they often show a preference for the latter. Whilst working in
a group they will be sought out by other pupils for their expertise and they are able to engage in
co-operative learning. They thrive on complexity and are much focused. Creativity plays a
major role their independent learning.

Disposition 2

These children are curious and will ask many questions. They prefer to learn by moving and
doing. They can see the big picture and will explore. They are kinaesthetic learners and
demonstrate this by their curiosity for taking things apart and putting them together again. They
want to be actively engaged in their learning environment, using visual and spatial awareness
and, as a consequence, they are very observant. They are often highly creative and enjoy
social interaction, but they can also be individualist. They often show leadership qualities.

Disposition 3

These children are easy to 'lose' in the classroom. They are quiet learners; often covertly able.
Although they may see the big picture they are focused, independent and sensitive. What they
know and understand will not always be as apparent as it is with the more verbal child. They do
not actively engage in their environs. Their sense of humour is more subtle and will be
expressed in their writing and speaking, often using puns and double meanings. They may
prefer to have their achievements quietly acknowledged.

Disposition 4

These are the social children of the group and are interactive learners. They enjoy sharing their
expertise with others and will be recognised by others for their leadership qualities. They are
hungry for attention. Their behaviour can often be misinterpreted as inappropriate or disruptive
and therefore their abilities may be missed.

© National Association for Able Children in Education - September 2006

NACE Early Years Able Learners: Indentification & Provision

Early Years Able Learners: Identification and Provision, adapted from Nebraska Starry
Night

know. Giving opportunities for parents to talk about how their children occupy themselves at home can help teachers make better judgements about their abilities.

Attention span can be one indicator of high ability – not, of course, watching the television for hours on end but becoming engaged in some worthwhile activity and being totally absorbed in it. Hours spent creating complex Lego models, drawing (not just colouring in), making up little plays, looking at books on particular topics, playing with numbers, can all be indicators of ability and parents are the people who will have noticed this absorption.

Case Study

Sean had not been to nursery or reception when he was living overseas with his parents but he and his younger siblings had led an exciting outdoor life and had visited several countries. He went directly into Year 1 when the family returned to the UK but did not settle well into his school, separating himself from other children and taking no part in early reading activities. He was restless and petulant. His teacher invited his mother in for a chat and was surprised to learn that Sean had pestered her to start reading when he was only 3 and was already enjoying books at night intended for 9–10-year-olds. Sean was also fascinated by wildlife and had to be discouraged from filling his bedroom with the insects he found in the garden. His mother brought in some of his paintings of butterflies and reptiles. With this information Sean's teacher, with the help of a teaching assistant and some children from KS2, was able to devise a teaching and learning programme more suitable for Sean's abilities.

Checklists

There are many checklists of characteristics that might indicate giftedness in children. These checklists tend to be quite similar but usually feature most of the following items:

1. Good problem solving/reasoning abilities
2. Very quick to learn
3. Early or avid reading ability
4. Advanced use of language
5. Wide range of interests
6. Long attention span when interested
7. Very observant/curious
8. Excellent memory
9. Great sense of humour
10. Empathetic
11. Strives for perfection
12. Intense

13. Interested in 'adult' matters
14. Prefers company of older students and adults
15. Concerned with justice, fairness
16. Sometimes judgement seems mature for age
17. Sensitive to hurt or criticism
18. Vivid imagination
19. High degree of creativity/originality
20. High degrees of energy
21. May challenge authority.

Although all checklists have to be treated with caution, they can be useful when groups of teachers are deciding which children should be included in a school's gifted and talented cohort. Such a list can focus discussion on the potentially gifted behaviours of particular children and might bring to light those who are not the most obvious candidates.

There are tests of general ability such as IQ tests that can be used with this age group but reliability is an issue for any group test, given the developmental problems mentioned earlier. Those tests that can be used on an individual basis by educational psychologists, such as WISC, can be very informative but this is a resource that few schools can afford for a whole year group of children. On any of these tests, a reasonable rule of thumb is if a child scores high take it seriously; if not, reserve judgement.

Identification at Key Stage 2 (ages 7–11)

KS1 Teacher Assessments

At this stage there are additional resources at the teacher's disposal. For a start there are KS1 teacher assessments in English and mathematics. Clearly those who achieve a Level 3 or even 4 are working above the expected level for that age group and teachers should have high expectations of them. In the UK, with the current concern about raising literacy and numeracy standards and fears about schools' positions in published league tables, there is a danger that schools will focus on these areas when selecting their gifted and talented cohort and that children whose abilities lie in other areas will be overlooked.

Tests of General Ability

Tests of general ability can be used more successfully with this age group as long as teachers bear in mind that some children will underperform because of nervousness or feeling unwell on the day or having worries about home that make it difficult for them to concentrate; or even because there are other things they would prefer to think or daydream about. These tests are less dependent on the teaching a child has received and provide a picture of underlying ability. As with all paper and pencil testing, the same rule applies as at KS1 – take seriously, act on very high scores and reserve judgement on others.

One test that is very popular in the UK is the Cognitive Abilities Test published by GL Assessment. There are three parts to CATs tests, which can be used with children from 7.5 years to 17+ – numerical or quantitative (QR), verbal (VR) and non-verbal (NVR). In many schools, the scores for the three sub-tests are aggregated and an average mark used as a basis for discussion or even decisions about grouping within a class or school. This can be a mistake because such an average would mask important strengths and weaknesses. For example, one local authority that used these tests for all Year 6 pupils, scrutinized the sub-test scores very closely and realized that non-verbal scores were markedly stronger for the cohort in general than verbal scores, suggesting that some kind of literacy intervention was required if these students were going to be able to make the most of their abilities. The table below also illustrates the importance of the individual scores of four Year 6 (age 11) students.

Name	Verbal Reasoning (VR)	Quantitative Reasoning (QR)	Non-Verbal Reasoning (NVR)	Average
Mandy	98	106	120	108
Jane	125	115	111	117
Peter	124	130	124	126
Fred	108	125	128	120
Guide to CATs Scores				
110+ most able 25% 114+ most able 20% 119+ most able 10% 126+ most able 5% Ceiling is 130				

Year 6 CATs Scores

By simply looking at the average scores, it might be decided that Peter and Fred should definitely be part of the gifted and talented cohort, that Jane might be considered and that Mandy was not a candidate. However, the scores on the sub-tests suggest that many more questions need to be asked, including:

1. Has Mandy's high NVR been reflected in work in art or design technology? Does her progress in these areas need to be monitored carefully?
2. Should Jane be included in the gifted and talented cohort on the basis of her strength in verbal reasoning?
3. As Peter's mathematics score is the ceiling for that test, is he being given work of an appropriate level in class or is he coasting?
4. As Fred's VR score is so much lower than those for QR and NVR, should this be investigated more carefully? Could it indicate a specific learning difficulty that has been overlooked until now?

Again, it needs to be stressed that test information of this kind should be used as part of an identification strategy and should not be allowed to become *the* strategy in its own right.

Out of School Interests

By the time children are in KS2, many of them have already established strong interests outside school. Ideally, any identification strategy should use information about these interests when drawing up a gifted and talented cohort. However, making contact with a disparate range of organizations can be time-consuming for schools. When meetings are arranged between teachers and parents it is rare for the right kinds of questions to be asked that encourage parents to talk about these activities and interests.

One school, recognizing the difficulty of gathering information of this kind, has special assemblies where children are presented with the awards they have gained such as cub and scout badges, instrumental music certificates, sports badges and dance qualifications. Parents are invited to submit information about awards and about achievements within the home, such as particularly good pieces of artwork, a story or an invention, and to attend these assemblies. This measure has proved to be very effective in drawing parents into the identification strategy and bridging the gap between the community and the school. Some organizations, on hearing about these award assemblies, have started to contact the school directly with information.

Peer- and Self-Nomination

At KS2, students are becoming more aware of themselves in relation to others and will have formed opinions about who in the class is good at particular things. Peer-nomination can be used quite discreetly by enquiring of a class which children should be asked for help with a particular task, with questions such as: Who would be able to help us to invent a new machine? Who should we ask to create a school website?

The same approach can be used to identify those children perceived to be leaders: Who would you like to lead you if you were lost in a jungle?

Self-nomination can also be explored if it is done in such away that students are not exposed to ridicule. For example, if a project of some kind is being organized, the teacher could identify a number of roles and skill areas and invite students to apply for them using a simple tick box. A class newspaper would require an editor, a team of journalists, photographers, feature writers with good interviewing and writing skills, advertising skills, someone with desktop publishing skills and internet researchers. Inviting children to suggest in confidence the roles they should take and being prepared to take a few risks when distributing the roles can be very revealing.

Teacher Observation

Teacher observation is an obvious identification tool. Very often a child who is underperforming in the classroom and on tests will be identified by the 'gut-feeling' of a particular teacher that there is great ability if only it can be drawn out. The student–teacher relationship is crucial to the identification and nurturing of gifts and talents. Winner (1996:144) draws attention to the research of Benjamin Bloom who found in his studies of world-class achievers that 'not one of his cases had achieved expertise without a supportive and encouraging environment, including a long and intensive period of training, first from loving and warm teachers, and then from rigorous and demanding master teachers'.

Over and over again one hears high-achieving adults ascribing their success to the inspiration of brilliant teachers or of teachers who, at least, recognized their gifts or talents and encouraged them to use them. Two words come up frequently – belief and expectation. Because these teachers seemed to believe in their abilities and had high expectations of what they could achieve, students found themselves raising their game and believing in themselves.

Different teachers will draw out different qualities in different children so it is important that teachers respect each other's assessments of potential if able children are not to fall through the net. There will be those who spot the poetry in a child's language, others who draw out the young politician or philosopher and yet others who see budding artists in doodles and graffiti.

Case Study

Peter had developed a reputation as the class clown by the time he moved into Year 6. Whenever the teacher addressed a question to him, his classmates would begin to giggle and Peter responded to his audience by joking and waving. His writing and spelling made his work almost indecipherable but he would write pages and pages when given the chance. More often than not, other teachers had read and corrected the first page and given up. Teachers were never sure whether he was very clumsy or if he knocked things off his desk and tripped over things intentionally. His new Year 6 teacher noted that his joking was quite accomplished with perfect comic timing. She also caught his apprehension when he brought another mammoth unreadable story to her desk. On one occasion she sent him off to a walk-in cupboard with a recorder and microphone and asked him to read his story into the recorder. Later, when she played it back, she realized that it was well structured and entertaining. She arranged for another child, who preferred to stay in at lunchtime rather than face the rough and tumble of the playground, to use the computer to transpose the story into print. This was the first of Peter's stories to be pinned on the classroom wall and his extreme delight was touching. His teacher then arranged an assessment with a visiting educational psychologist, who found that he was of well above average ability with particularly strong verbal skills. He was also both dyslexic and dyspraxic. Peter was placed on both the SEN and gifted and talented registers. A remedial programme was put in place for him while, at the same time, his teacher fostered his love of story and play writing by introducing him to a wide range of children's books and encouraging him to use the computer for his compositions. He wrote a play that was performed by his classmates to the rest of the school.

Although teacher nomination is important, it should never be the only means of identification because, as with all the other strategies, it is an imperfect tool. Teachers tend to pick the same sort of students over and over again and miss others entirely. Research in England by Bennet et al., quoted by Joan Freeman (1998:8), found that 40 per cent of potentially high achievers had been underestimated by their teachers. Equally worrying, Nebesnuik found 'a significant discrepancy between the assessment of able pupils by their primary teachers and subsequently by Year 7 teachers'. Sometimes generalist teachers in primary schools fail to notice abilities in specialist subjects but it is equally true that specialist teachers in secondary schools may be oblivious to students' abilities outside their subject expertise.

Identification in the Secondary School – Key Stages 3–5 (ages 11–19)

When students enter secondary school it is quite common for a mass of quantitative and qualitative data to arrive with them – KS2 SATs, CAT scores, profiles, teacher recommendations, bridging projects and samples of work. Unfortunately, for many and varied reasons, the available data is not always used. Sometimes this is because the primary/secondary liaison teacher does not pass it on to departments and sometimes it is intentionally ignored in the belief that all students should start afresh in their new school. The outcome is that many students have to go through the whole process of proving their ability yet again. The dip in achievement of able students in Year 7 is well recorded. Some are so disheartened by being set low-level tasks that they give up trying and continue to underperform throughout the rest of their schooling.

Group Assessments

In spite of this plethora of information, some schools decide to carry out further group assessments. This is understandable in schools accepting children from primary schools in several local authorities where there has been no standardization of testing beyond SATs and no consistency in the kind of information provided. The assessments used in Year 7 might be CATs, if not done in Year 6, or MidYIS tests, which are designed to measure aptitude for learning and ability. The main tests cover vocabulary, mathematics, verbal and non-verbal skills and can be used by schools to predict performance in public examinations and to identify gifted students. As long as these tests do not become the sole identification tool, they are a valuable source of information as part of a pupil profile.

Indicators of Underachievement

Even in primary schools, it is not uncommon for the climate to be so hostile to academic ability that students learn at an early age to keep their heads down and to underachieve. In secondary schools the climate can be even more threatening and the perceived need to play down abilities greater. This is particularly true of some inner city schools but is certainly not exclusive to them. When looking for evidence of high ability in these circumstances, teachers need also to be aware of some of the indicators of underachievement. There are a number of checklists of characteristics of underachievers. The one below is a modified version of one produced by Joanne Whitmore (1980). She suggests that if, over the course of a couple of weeks, a student exhibits ten of these behaviours, including all those that are starred, further sophisticated testing of general ability should be considered to establish whether or not s/he is a gifted or talented underachiever.

✓	Checklist to Identify Gifted Underachievers
	Performs badly on tests of attainment
	Achieves at or below expected levels in literacy or mathematics
	Daily work is often unfinished or poorly executed
	When interested, shows superior comprehension and ability to absorb information
	Vast gap between level of spoken and written work
	Tries to avoid new activities because of fear of failure. Self-critical and inclined to perfectionism
	Has a wide range of interests and even specialist expertise in one or more fields
	Low self-esteem demonstrated through aggression or withdrawal in the classroom
	Not comfortable doing group work
	Has few friends. Poor relationship with peers
	Resists teacher's efforts to motivate or discipline
	Poor concentration. Easily distracted
	Indifferent or negative attitude to school
	Exceptionally large repertoire of factual knowledge
	Imaginative and creative
	May show initiative in completing self-selected projects at home
	Has unrealistic expectations. Often sets goals too high or too low
	Always dissatisfied with the work s/he produces
	Dislikes rote learning and practising skills for mastery
	Extremely sensitive and perceptive about self, others and life in general

Case Study

Yasmin in Year 8 made it very difficult for her teachers to reach her. Hostility emanated from her as soon as she entered the classroom. Her frequent absences from school were a cause for concern but the more honest teachers admitted that they gave a sigh of relief when she was not there. The gentlest of criticisms about lack of homework or poor quality work provoked a torrent of self-justification. When she was persuaded into group work, there usually came a point when she would storm away because she was unable to compromise. And yet there were also times when Yasmin was totally absorbed, usually in English, history or RE when the teacher was telling a story. She mocked organized religion and politicians but was very well informed and relished debate. Although unwilling to stick to the rules of formal debating she was a formidable opponent. Sometimes she would be so inspired by a topic that she would settle down in class to write at length but she would give up as soon as she re-read her work and decided that it did not live up to her expectations.

After many complaints from her teachers, her head of year called a meeting to review her progress. When they looked back over the data received from primary school including CAT

→ continued . . .

scores, they realized that she was seriously underachieving. The school was fortunate to have a home/school liaison officer who acted as a link where parents were unwilling to come into the school. She visited the home and found that Yasmin was acting as a carer to her mother, who had mental health problems, and her two younger siblings. Her father had left some time ago. Yasmin was angry and embarrassed when the liaison officer arrived. She did not want anyone at school to see the conditions in which she was living and was also afraid that she would be taken into care if the authorities realized that she was the primary carer. It took some weeks for the liaison officer to break through this distrust so that she could contact social services and arrange for some support to be offered to the mother and Yasmin. One of the English teachers, who had a good relationship with her, agreed to act as a mentor and meet her at regular intervals. Together they set a series of manageable targets to build up her confidence. It took two years of patience on the part of teachers and mentor to bring Yasmin's work up to standard. Yasmin also had to work hard to control her tendency to be defensive and prickly. Her relationship with her peers began to improve and she began to have higher aspirations.

Subject Specialists

At secondary level the subject specialist has an extremely important role to play in the identification of gifted and talented students. Some students only 'switch on' in a few lessons. It is the subject teacher who will spot this interest and enthusiasm and who should bring it to the attention of the departmental head and gifted and talented lead teacher. The enthusiastic computer technologist, who communicates as an equal with his design technology teacher, may be passive and unresponsive for most of the school day. The science teacher may be the one who notices a student's acute observations and fascination with all things scientific, while the MFL teacher might pick up a quiet student's ready facility with a new language. It is essential that individual specialist teachers' assessments of high potential are included in the equation when a school's gifted and talented cohort is being put together.

Some school departments or faculties will be looking for quite specific behaviours in high ability students and may have devised strategies to identify these abilities. For example, PE and sports departments are becoming increasingly well organized in their approach to identifying and developing potential. Some schools send a specialist into primary schools to carry out a battery of skill-related tests with Year 6 pupils. When they join their secondary school they can be grouped appropriately and where outstanding potential has been identified it can be nurtured. Others carry out similar screening when students enter secondary school. In some cases, the assess-intervene-assess approach described earlier in this chapter is used on a skill-by-skill basis and gradually profiles of all students' abilities are compiled.

Some departments draw up their own subject-specific checklists of character-istics of students who are likely to be able in their subjects. It is never a good idea to simply copy another school's checklist into a departmental policy because it is the discussion that takes place within a department when the checklist is being compiled that is really valuable, rather than the list itself. So often it reveals very different perceptions among teachers of what constitutes high potential and helps to ensure that they are looking for similar characteristics. A useful exercise when these different perceptions are problematic is to invite all the teachers in a department to bring along a piece of outstanding work to a meeting, so that the qualities being sought can be highlighted and irrelevancies identified.

When students enter KS4 (ages 14–16) and KS5 (ages 16–19), some of those who have kept a low profile, because they feared that their interests and abilities would make them stand out in a crowd, become more confident to be themselves. Others are more motivated when they are allowed to specialize and to spend more time with students who have similar interests. This is when quite outstanding abilities begin to emerge. It is also the stage at which leadership opportunities become more plentiful and some students grow into these and demonstrate skills that have been overlooked.

In the radio programme *Desert Island Discs* (28 December 2007), Victoria Wood – comedienne, playwright and songwriter – described how she was isolated and underachieving in her grammar school until she was 15, when Rochdale Council set up a youth theatre. From the day she joined, she felt that she belonged. In this climate she was able to develop her latent talents and begin to deal with her insecurities. One has to wonder what would have happened to her if this opportunity had not come along.

The key message is that gifts and talents can emerge at any age and any stage and that a wide range of strategies should be used to build up a profile of a student including:

- provision-based assessment
- standardized tests, SATs and public examinations
- screening information such as the Foundation Stage Profile
- school- and classroom-based assessments
- teacher observation and nomination
- parent-, peer- and self-nomination
- general- and subject-specific checklists
- information from external organizations.

Identification of the Hard to Assess

There are several groups of students whose abilities can be hard to assess and whose gifts or talents can so easily be overlooked. These include children with physical and communication problems, those with behavioural or social problems and those for whom English is an additional language. Obviously teacher observation, the starry night profile and identification by provision are still very important for these groups but standardized tests of the kind described earlier are unlikely to be useful.

There are a number of other tests that can be used to throw light on their underlying abilities. These include the Raven's Coloured Progressive Matrices and the British Picture Vocabulary Scale.

Case Study

A learning support specialist was invited to a school for boys with serious behaviour problems. The headteacher explained that she had a group of four boys between the ages of 9 and 12 who intrigued her. None of them could read and they were very disturbed but she was convinced that their underlying ability was very high and she was looking for evidence of this. The learning support specialist used the Raven's Coloured Progressive Matrices to assess each boy's reasoning skills. The advantage of this test is that no reading or spoken communication is required. Students simply identify by pointing to the missing piece of a design. The designs become more complex as the test advances. The scores of three of the four boys put them in the top 10 per cent of the ability range. With this information the headteacher felt more confident of exploring ways to harness this ability.

The Coloured Progressive Matrices can also be very useful for EAL students, because scores are not affected greatly by linguistic and cultural backgrounds and can be a useful predictor of success. It could also be used with students who have no speech and very limited movement.

Case Study

A child in an infant school, whom teachers suspected had been a victim of some kind of abuse, elected to be mute. She sat in the same place in the classroom day after day ignoring her peers and refusing to take part in any activity. The teacher did notice, however, that she looked up and listened at story time. On the advice of an educational psychologist, the teacher sat down with the child and gradually persuaded her to take part in the British Picture Vocabulary Scale. As the rest of the class was in the hall with another teacher, the child seemed to enjoy the one-to-one attention. In this test, there are four pictures on each page. The teacher says a trigger word and the child simply has to point at the picture she associates with the word. The language becomes more complex as the test develops. Even though the teacher had suspected that the child was quite able, she was taken aback by the high level of comprehension identified by the test and sought further help from specialists.

National Quality Standards for Gifted and Talented Education

Identification of high ability in our schools is a much more sophisticated process than it was when 11+ tests reigned supreme and the skills being identified were very limited. However, it is still important that as many people as possible are involved in the process and that schools never stop assessing and reassessing potential.

All schools in England should be using the Institutional Quality Standards for Gifted and Talented Education (IQS) (see Appendix 1) and Classroom Quality Standards (CQS) to assess their progress in providing for gifted and talented students, including the development of sound identification strategies. Schools in other countries would also find these useful. When planning how to improve, for example, identification of high ability, schools first use the criteria for each Standard to assess their current practice. If it appears to be Entry Level, they can then draw up an action plan for moving forward to the Developing Level and eventually to the Exemplary Level. It is worth noting here that schools aspiring to the highest of the three Standards in Identification – Exemplary – need to show that:

- **Multiple criteria** and **sources of evidence** are used to identify gifts and talents, including through the use of a broad range of quantitative and qualitative data.
- The record is supported by a comprehensive monitoring, progress planning and report system, which all staff regularly share and contribute to.
- **Identification** processes are regularly reviewed and refreshed in the light of pupil performance and value-added data. The gifted and talented population is fully representative of the school/college's population.

3 School-wide Strategies for Supporting Gifted and Talented Children

School Culture

During his premiership, Tony Blair often reiterated his priorities for the nation – Education, Education, Education. He might well have added Expectation, Expectation, Expectation to his mantra because teachers and parents with high expectations and belief in success hold the key to unlocking potential in students of all ages. At present it is fashionable to stress the importance of raising children's self-esteem and there is a whole industry devoted to this, but there is little scientific evidence about the efficacy of most of the strategies being adopted. According to Professor Nicholas Emler, who conducted a review of research on self-esteem for the Joseph Rowntree Trust, parents and genetic makeup are the strongest influences upon self-esteem. He also concluded that: 'relatively low self-esteem is not a risk factor for delinquency, violence towards others (including child and partner abuse), drug use, alcohol abuse, *educational under-attainment* or racism'. (Joseph Rowntree Foundation 2001) On the other hand, changing teachers' and parents' expectations has been shown over and over again (look at Ofsted reports) to be the driver behind school improvement and improved pupil achievement.

Many schools have pockets of excellence – a stunning reception teacher who instinctively recognizes those children who are already achieving well ahead of their peers and is able to stimulate them; a vibrant art department that encourages students to work in a wide range of media, regularly takes groups out to art galleries, is heavily used by students during the lunch hours and after school and puts on magnificent displays around the building; or an innovative science team that really captures the enthusiasm of students, uses computer technology to good effect, runs an after-school chemistry club, takes part in local competitions and so on – but it can be the case that such departments flourish in spite of the overall school culture in relation to gifted and talented students rather than because of it.

Headteachers may find themselves taking over schools and teachers may find themselves teaching in schools where:

1. The atmosphere is so macho that it is acceptable for keen footballers to be cheered as they posture on the stage after winning a coveted cup but no academically able student would dare to accept an award in front of the same audience for winning a maths or writing competition.
2. The curriculum is presented in such a way that girls flourish and boys underachieve. This can be a particular problem in primary schools with an all female teaching staff.
3. Academic success is prized above everything else and talents such as art, music, sport or drama are sadly neglected. This neglect can also happen in schools so fearful of losing their place in league tables that they concentrate only on what is tested.
4. Students from certain ethnic and social groups are not expected to achieve.
5. There are key personalities in the staffroom who actively inhibit cultural change in relation to gifted and talented students.
6. Parents who suggest that more should be expected of their children are dismissed as pushy parents.

If a school is to make good provision for its gifted and talented students, it first needs to take a long honest look at its prevailing culture and, if there are problems, explore ways of changing it.

Nurturing Schools

A school is most likely to provide a nurturing environment in which all gifts and talents can flourish if:

1. The senior management team is committed to making good provision for these children and actively promotes innovation and good practice. Goodhew (2004), reporting on a DfES gifted and talented initiative involving Schools Facing Challenging Circumstances, found that the attitude of senior management was the key factor in determining the success of the project in individual schools.
2. Expectations of all children, no matter what their ethnicity, religious creed or gender, are high.
3. Stereotyping is discouraged so that, for example, Black boys are expected to have the same academic aspirations as other students.
4. There is a can-do approach amongst teachers such that it is rare to hear them say 'you can't expect much from children like these'.
5. All gifts and talents are accorded equal status.
6. Achievement of all sorts is regularly celebrated in a variety of ways and students are encouraged to be proud of each other's achievements.
7. Parents are involved in the identification and support of gifted and talented students.
8. A strong anti-bullying policy is in place and teachers are discouraged from 'putting down' able students.
9. Partnerships with other schools and outside organizations are exploited to provide additional support and learning opportunities for able students.
10. The school is receptive to new ideas.
11. Approaches to grouping are flexible.

Changing a school's culture can be tricky because it can be so difficult from the inside to see what is going wrong. Taking a look at some of the school's data or a group of schools' data relating to achievement is often a good starting point.

Case Study

The gifted and talented coordinators from four secondary schools in a poor White area of England met up and put together the results of their most able students for GCSE English, maths and science. After discussing the findings they began to explore ways of supporting each other to raise standards.

Science GCSE Grades A*–B

	Boys %				Girls %			
	A*	A	B	A*–B	A*	A	B	A*–B
School A		12	15.2	**27.2**		7.3	19.5	**26.8**
School B	1.5	2.9	5.9	**10.3**	1.6		6.3	**7.9**
School C		4.7	1.6	**6.3**		3.1	14.1	**17.2**
School D			9.5	**9.5**	2.2	4.3	6.5	**13**
Schools' Mean	**0.4**	**4.9**	**8.1**	**13.4**	**1.0**	**3.7**	**11.6**	**16.2**

English GCSE Grades A*–B

	Boys %				Girls %			
	A*	A	B	A*–B	A*	A	B	A*–B
School A	1.3	6.7	18.7	**26.7**		7.4	19.8	**27.2**
School B	1.5	2.9	5.9	**10.3**	1.5	6.2	24.6	**32.3**
School C		3.3	14.8	**18.1**	1.6	9.7	22.6	**33.9**
School D			2	**2**		6	12	**18**
Schools' Mean	**0.7**	**3.2**	**10.4**	**14.3**	**0.8**	**7.3**	**19.8**	**27.9**

Mathematics GCSE Grades A*–B

	Boys %				Girls %			
	A*	A	B	A*–B	A*	A	B	A*–B
School A	1.2	3.6	17.9	**22.7**		2.3	13.8	**16.1**
School B		5.9	5.9	**11.8**	1.6	1.6	18.8	**22**
School C	1.6	3.2	6.3	**11.1**		1.8	25	**26.8**
School D		7.1	14.3	**21.4**	2.1	8.3	18.8	**29.2**
Schools' Mean	**0.7**	**5.0**	**11.1**	**16.7**	**1.0**	**3.5**	**19.1**	**23.5**

This exercise provoked a number of questions:

→ continued . . .

1. Why, in comparison with other areas, were the results still low?

2. Why was underachievement among boys in all schools apart from School A such a problem?

3. Why was this problem especially pronounced in English?

4. Looking at the percentage of A*–B in English, why was the performance of girls in Schools B and C so relatively strong?

5. School D's mathematics results are easily the best but its performance in both English and science was very weak. What was different about the mathematics department in that school?

6. School A appeared to have closed the performance gap between boys and girls. How had it done this?

The coordinators set up a number of meetings between teachers in their science, mathematics and English departments, and arranged visits to schools outside the area that were notably successful in dealing with male underachievement. Some after-school CPD was organized. They also used the results of a Keele University Pupil Survey to get a better understanding of pupils' perceptions of school life and to pinpoint factors that could be contributing to underachievement. All the information was fed back to the senior management team of each school so that action plans could be developed and suitable measures taken. (Keele University 2005)

Gifted and Talented Policy

With schools in England now being expected to identify their gifted and talented pupils as part of the annual schools' census so that their progress can be monitored on a national basis, it is no longer possible to 'opt out' of developing a coherent policy for these students.

Is a written gifted and talented policy needed? Quite honestly, as with subject checklists mentioned in the previous chapter, the process of meeting and agreeing as a whole school how the needs of these students are to be met is much more important than the final document. What should be avoided at all costs is the practice of copying a gifted and talented policy from another school or from a book, changing the names and presenting it as school policy. It will simply moulder in a drawer and will have no impact on practice. Provision for gifted and talented students may already be incorporated into other school policies such as teaching and learning or inclusion. There is no point in creating another document if this is the case.

However, working together on a gifted and talented policy can be really helpful where a school is more or less starting from scratch with this issue or when it is unhappy with current provision and wants to make radical changes. Provision for able students should be seen as part of a school's approach to inclusion and must fit in with overall school policy and philosophy. A gifted and talented policy cannot be produced overnight and should never be written by one person without consulting other colleagues. This is another circumstance in which the policy ends up ignored and eventually forgotten. Ideally everyone in a school should make a contribution. The more teachers that are involved, the greater the impact it is likely to have. It will also need to develop and change over time as circumstances change and as the school becomes more sophisticated in its approach to able children.

When drawing up a policy, the following questions should be addressed:

1. What do the terms gifted and talented or able mean as they are applied in the school?
2. Why do you need a policy and how does it link with other policies such as inclusion?
3. How will high ability be identified and the progress of these students monitored?
4. Who will be responsible for implementing and updating the policy? This should not simply be left to the lead teacher for gifted and talented education or the headteacher. Of course, one person will have to take ultimate responsibility for making sure that the gifted and talented cohort is updated and, in England, their details entered on the annual PLASC census. However, there should be input from all teachers in primary schools and all departments in secondary settings. Pastoral staff should also be contributing relevant information and making suggestions as to how the policy could be improved. It is essential that the policy is dynamic, not fixed in stone, and that all teachers believe it is their policy and not one that has been foisted on them.
5. How will able students' needs be met in the classroom? The grouping of students both at classroom and school level will need to be considered here as well as how the necessary challenge will be provided. Assessment of learning and for learning might also be mentioned here.
6. How will able students be supported when they move into the school or transfer to another school?
7. How will able students' social and emotional needs be met? Will mentoring be considered? Remember that a policy should reflect what is happening in the school and not what would happen in ideal circumstances. If a school is not yet ready to consider mentoring or any other form of provision then it should be left out or mentioned as a consideration for the future.
8. What opportunities will there be beyond the classroom? For example, are there any links with organizations operating the Extended School Day and do they organize activities that are particularly beneficial to the most able?
9. How will outside agencies and parents be involved? There is an expectation that schools in England will encourage students to become involved in the regional activities offered by Young, Gifted and Talented (YGT).
10. How will the success of the policy be evaluated?

Coordinating Approaches to Gifted and Talented Students

Every school in England is expected to have a leading teacher for gifted and talented education. There are two important aspects of their role, namely to lead:

- 'whole-school self-evaluation and improvement planning for gifted and talented provision and outcomes
- effective classroom practice for gifted and talented pupils'. (DfES 2007:44)

An important difference between leading teachers and the gifted and talented coordinators they have replaced is that leading teachers are expected to *exemplify* best practice for gifted and talented learners in the classroom. The emphasis has moved from having all the documentation, such as policies and gifted and talented registers, in place to getting classroom provision right. Since appropriate provision is central to meeting the needs of able students this is clearly a good move, as long as suitable teachers can be found to undertake this role. Small schools may have to explore ways of working in clusters with a 'cluster leading teacher'. However, financing such an initiative might be problematic. Ideally, the leading teacher in every school will need to be a well-respected or senior teacher otherwise it will be very difficult for them to approach their peers about implementing effective pedagogy or suggesting coaching in relation to teaching able students.

Institutional Quality Standards (IQS) for Gifted and Talented Education

A useful tool for senior managers and leading teachers seeking to improve a school's approach to gifted and talented education is IQS, devised by the Department for Children, Schools and Families (dcsf) in association with teachers and other interested parties. It is, in essence, a self-evaluation tool that helps schools to assess their progress towards excellent gifted and talented provision. There are three levels – Entry, Developing and Exemplary. Schools can use IQS in several ways, but many choose to:

- identify where they are in each of the generic elements
- choose one or more priorities
- draw up an action plan

- implement the action plan
- assess the success of this action
- modify the approach if necessary or move on to another element or another level and repeat the process.

A school may also choose to concentrate on just one element, for example, leadership. The three levels for this component are:

School/College Organization – Leadership	
Entry	A named member of the governing body, senior management team and the lead professional responsible for gifted and talented education have clearly directed responsibilities for motivating and driving gifted and talented provision. The headteacher actively champions gifted and talented provision.
Developing	**Responsibility** for gifted and talented provision is **distributed** and evaluation of its impact shared at all levels in the school/college. Staff subscribe to policy at all levels. Governors play a significant supportive and evaluative role.
Exemplary	Organizational structures, communication channels and the deployment of staff (e.g. workforce remodelling) are flexible and creative in supporting the delivery of personalized learning. Governors take a lead in celebrating achievement of gifted and talented pupils.

The differences between the school at Entry Level that is putting structures and personnel in place and a school that has the confidence to use staff and structures in a flexible way to achieve its goals and personalize learning are very obvious.

Progress with the various elements of IQS (see Appendix 1) can be used as evidence when completing a school's Ofsted Self-Evaluation Form.

Grouping/Organizational Strategies and Gifted and Talented Students

One factor affecting the opportunities and performance of potentially gifted students is a school's approach to grouping and organization of the school day. The strategies adopted by individual primary and secondary schools will depend to some extent on the size of the schools and the resources available to them. A small primary school with fewer than ten students in each year group cannot easily consider fine setting although it could group children across two or more years. Similarly a two-form entry secondary school will be more limited in the grouping strategies it can try than a ten-form entry school.

The pros and cons of the various groupings are well rehearsed but it is worth re-iterating the health warnings and opportunities associated with some of them.

Grouping Strategies in Primary and Secondary Schools	
Pros	Cons
Streaming, where students are given some kind of general assessment and then placed in the same ability group for all lessons.	
Can be very stimulating for those who happen to be able all-rounders.	Thankfully less common than it used to be. Students whose performance is more uneven, possibly with poor verbal skills but good mathematical ability, languish in the lower streams and do not have the chance to show what they are capable of achieving because teacher expectations of these classes may not be high.
Setting, where pupils are grouped according to ability on a subject-by-subject basis.	
This allows students to be in groups appropriate to their different abilities. It should be relatively easy to move students from one set to another depending on the progress they make.	Students of all abilities can suffer if this approach is adhered to too rigidly. Low teacher expectation is a problem for all children in the lower sets. Those who are late developers may find it very difficult to move up the sets because of teacher reluctance to move others out of the top sets to make space for them. There are particular dangers when setting is used in infant and junior schools. The problems of the 'young in year' children and those who mature more slowly were mentioned in Chapter 2 and can be exacerbated if they get stuck in lower sets at an early stage and learn to live down to expectation.
Mixed ability grouping is the norm in primary schools and is used in many secondary schools, especially in English and the humanities, or in Years 7 and 8.	
Late developers are not discouraged. Mixing with the full ability and social spectrum in a school helps able students to become more rounded and aware individuals. It can also raise the achievement of less able students because the gifted and talented will ask questions that encourage others to think more deeply.	There is a tendency for teachers to teach to the average child and not provide sufficient challenge and stimulation for the more able. It is rare when looking at lesson, topic or unit plans to find details of how the most able will be moved forward in their learning. Very often, there will be a reference to targeted questions or referring them to more challenging materials but for the most part it is simple tokenism.
Express classes, usually slightly smaller than other groups, where students remain with their peer group but move through the curriculum at a faster pace and even sit external tests and exams early. Sometimes this grouping occurs for all lessons and sometimes only for mathematics, MFL or other subjects.	
Can provide a very stimulating environment for the very able. Teachers can set a good pace and explore topics in greater depth. Within the classroom, able children are more protected and can show their abilities.	The pace might not be appropriate for those at the bottom end of the express group. Careful long-term planning is required so that there is an appropriate programme of work after tests and exams have been taken early. Can be difficult to move late developers into such a group.

Pros	Cons
Vertical or family grouping. Students from several year groups are placed in one tutor group and remain in this group throughout their time at the school. In primary schools children may have all their lessons in this group but not in secondary schools.	
A secure learning environment in primary schools where very able young children have the stimulation of older children in the group. Teachers get to know children very well and can bring them on at their own pace.	Not very challenging for able older children. Difficult for teachers to meet the needs of such a broad age and ability range.
Flexible grouping. Some schools are experimenting with flexible grouping where students have a home base for a subject but they are regularly regrouped across the year for different activities.	
Gives teachers a huge range of grouping possibilities including ability grouping for particular skills within a subject.	Older students are unsettled by frequent changes of grouping. This demands high energy levels from teachers. They have to get to know many more children.
Grouping by gender	
Some schools report that girls are more successful in sciences and mathematics when there are no boys in the group. Similarly, boys often appear to underachieve in subjects like English and modern foreign languages when girls are present. Teachers can also introduce a more competitive climate to a classroom if only boys are present. They appear to respond to this approach.	Several schools have tried this on a short-term basis and reported successful outcomes both in terms of pupil response and test results but for some reason, few seem to pursue it in the long term.
Extracting small groups for targeted work	
One secondary school sends a letter home to all Year 7 parents explaining that at some point during the year, all pupils will be working in a small group. The school can then use this as an opportunity to draw very able students together for a particular topic or purpose. If necessary, they can group across years. Some primary schools are adopting a similar approach.	Careful planning and liaison with all teachers is needed to make sure that best use is made of this time.

A flexible approach to timetabling may have to be used where schools have, or wish to foster, a particular population of gifted or talented pupils.

Case Study

'Through the work of Karl Wharton, a former teacher at the school and now a national gymnastics coach, Deerness Valley has attracted so many young gymnasts that they have been able to set up special tutor groups for them in Years 7 and 8. This provision allows them all to train at the High Performance Centre from 7.30 a.m. before starting their school programme slightly later. Research has suggested that pupils, whose talents are supported by sensitive provision of this sort, perform well in public examinations.' (Goodhew 2004:18)

Acceleration

Acceleration is used here to mean moving individuals or groups of students out of their peer group and up a year or more so that they are working at a more advanced stage of the curriculum. In the case of primary age children this could mean early transfer to secondary school and for secondary age students it can mean completing schooling a year or more early. It is an approach that goes in and out of favour and there can be little doubt that there are some students for whom it is very helpful. But it can also have dire consequences when used inappropriately. Joan Freeman, in her longitudinal study of a group of gifted students in North West England, found that:

> While at school, it could be seen that very few had benefited from being accelerated. Seventeen of the Follow-up's 169 young people had either been accelerated or were young for their class. Many had found this presented them with such difficulties that they were at times detrimental to their greater well-being. Paradoxically, acceleration may even have been responsible, as some parents thought, for lowering their children's final examination marks.
> (Freeman 2001:187)

Problems occur with acceleration for a number of reasons:

1. Although intellectually able, some young people do not have the physical, emotional or social maturity to cope with working in a class of older students. They may feel threatened and isolated. Sometimes they feel physically inadequate when they compare themselves with classmates.
2. The students themselves are not always fully consulted. Either teachers or teachers and parents make the decision for them.
3. Children are accelerated through primary school but do not feel confident to transfer to the secondary school early. They then have to repeat Year 6. Sometimes secondary schools are reluctant to accept younger children.
4. Tensions occur between gifted students and their parents when they want to do something which is appropriate for older classmates but not for them; for example, a 14-year-old in a sixth form might want to go to a nightclub with others from his/her teaching group.
5. Students who sit their A Levels early but are not ready to go to university at 16 or 17 often find themselves marking time for a year or two when insufficient thought has been given to post-examination programmes of study.
6. With the focus so firmly on achievement, social development is not always as satisfactory as it is for students who remain with their peers.

As schools are currently being encouraged to consider acceleration as part of the personalization agenda, there follow two cases studies; in one, the outcomes were positive, the other one less so. Appendix 2 is a checklist for teachers or parents who are considering accelerating a student or students.

Case Study

Dominic was our first (and only) child and we had little, if any, previous contact with small children. It therefore did not seem to us unusual that he knew the numbers by 10 months and the alphabet at 16 months of age. We read to him daily from a few weeks old and he learnt to read at home before going to school.

He started formal school at $4^1/_2$ and quickly settled down. By 5 Dominic found longer books more interesting and devoured as many as we could give him including numerous *Famous Five* books and *Swallows and Amazons*. A week after starting his second year, the head-master asked me to come into the school to discuss moving Dominic up a year. The school had carried out extensive testing and felt that he would be happier and more challenged in the year above. We talked about this suggestion at great length. We had both had the experience of skipping years at school.

Although neither of us had any personal problems being a year ahead, the difficulty was that at some point it is necessary to 'lose' the year. I repeated Year 6 and my husband took the 7th term Oxbridge Entrance examination. However, as we knew Dominic would move from this school to another at age 7 or 8 we felt we could always adjust his year group at that stage if necessary. We explained this to Dominic who was happy to comply once he knew where the new toilets were – that being his only concern. He maintained friendships from his old year group as well as making new friends in the new class.

In fact Dominic was able to start his new school a year early too, where he stayed until the end of Year 13. His age was never an issue, especially as he was tall and did not appear to be younger than his classmates. Dominic kept a good group of friends and did well socially and academically. If there were any social problems it was because he did not enjoy ball games. However, once he started rowing, this passed. He took GCSEs and A Levels early and moved on to Cambridge to study maths.

Whilst at senior school Dominic was not challenged by any of the work and found stimulation outside school with music – he achieved a performer's certificate at 15 – and with maths and physics Olympiads.

The age issue was only a problem with his application to Bristol University who would accept him on the course but not allow him to stay in university accommodation or go to the Union. Unsurprisingly he rejected their offer of a place. Cambridge University, where he now studies, had no problem accepting a young student and he is now 'fulfilled', challenged and happy in his world.

In conclusion, moving up a year was not necessarily a complete solution but it was better than not moving!

(Case study provided by Pamela Benson, mother of an exceptionally able student.)

$\longrightarrow$ *continued . . .*

Note:

1. Parents and child were consulted and given time to consider the issue.

2. Areas of anxiety (the toilets!) were dealt with.

3. The school and university he moved on to agreed to accept him even though he was young.

4. Dominic was sociable, confident and tall for his age and did not appear young within his new class.

5. He was encouraged to broaden his interests through out-of-school activities.

Case Study

Alice is 9 and an only child. Her parents are academics at a nearby university. Her teacher reports that she has very good literacy skills, having almost completed Level 5 in the National Curriculum, but does not like to think for herself. She is good at computation but does not respond well to other forms of maths.

The teacher's main worry about Alice concerns parental pressure. From the time Alice was in the first year, the parents were making suggestions that she ought to move on one year. They have been very persistent and determined to get their own way. The pressure came to a head last summer term when the parents again suggested that Alice move on. The school felt this was not in Alice's best interest, especially as she was young within the year, but eventually agreed to accelerate her to Year 6.

The current situation is worrying. Alice is now split from her best friend and they are beginning to drift apart. She already had difficulty in forming relationships and is therefore feeling isolated by her present classmates, who feel she is too young and make fun of her because of her flamboyant mannerisms. She has resorted to playing with children in Year 4. A decision has still to be reached about whether Alice transfers to secondary school a year early or not. No matter what happens now, the school feels she is in a 'no-win' situation. She apparently is feeling nervous and apprehensive about the proposed move and yet she could end up in the same class as the children she has moved from.

From Alice's point of view, she feels she is not struggling with any work. She has been concentrating on improving her handwriting. She plays the guitar, the recorder and the piano. She also takes French and goes to Brownies.

Note:

1. There was no consensus on the wisdom of this move.

2. Her overall level of ability does not appear to justify acceleration.

→ continued . . .

3. Alice does not appear to be particularly confident or socially adept, which could explain why some of her new classmates do not accept her.

4. It is not clear whether Alice understood that she might be required to move to secondary school before her peers.

Compacting the Curriculum

The Year 7 dip in the performance of able students is familiar to teachers and parents. There are a number of possible causes:

- Low teacher expectation. There is a tendency to under-estimate what new entrants to secondary schools can achieve. Students themselves often report being 'babied'.
- Lack of continuity and progression between primary and secondary schools.
- Because students come from a variety of primary schools with different strengths and weaknesses, teachers find it convenient to repeat work covered in Year 6 just to be on the safe side – understandable but very frustrating for pupils who were expecting to start on new and exciting work.
- A failure to make good use of the data provided by primary schools.
- The disorientation experienced by many Year 7 students when they find themselves in large and unfamiliar buildings and expected to cope with complex timetables and new rules.

Schools have experimented with many approaches to overcome the problem, including Year 6/7 summer schools for gifted and talented students; moving pupils from primary to secondary school in July so that they are settled in and a part of the school before the summer break; bridging units of work started in the primary school and continued in the receiving school; and two-way teacher exchanges between primary and secondary schools.

A more radical approach designed specifically for the most able pupils is that of curriculum compacting. Curriculum compacting involves:

- identifying learning objectives
- assessing the prior knowledge of students in relation to these learning objectives
- cutting out all unnecessary teaching or repetition of skills/knowledge already acquired.

There are several variations on this theme at school level (rather than at classroom level) but the most common approach is to compress the three-year KS3 curriculum into two years. Bearing in mind that able students need pace, breadth and depth in the curriculum to meet their learning needs, this strategy injects much more *pace* and the year that is freed up can be used in a number of different ways. Whether or not this approach is successful depends on how the problems associated with any kind of acceleration are tackled and how much consideration is given to the time freed up. A gallop through the KS3, followed by a similar gallop through KS4 and possibly even

KS5 is not very rewarding for students or teachers – apart from any satisfaction gained from getting to the finishing post first. On the other hand if the time is used to introduce *breadth* into the curriculum for able students by, for example, introducing additional languages or separate sciences at an earlier stage or even giving more time to subjects that tend to be squeezed in (drama or theatre studies) or are currently not included (philosophy, classics, astronomy, politics), then it can be worthwhile. The time could also be used to explore topics just touched on in the National Curriculum in greater *depth*.

Some primary and secondary schools compact the curriculum in such a way that a day a week or a month is freed up rather than a whole year.

Day a Week School (DWS) is an organization that helps clusters of schools looking to develop this kind of approach for students of exceptional ability. See NACE (2006) and Chapter 5 for a case study.

Assessment for Learning

Traditionally, assessment is something that comes at the end of a process – a score for a spelling test or grades for end of term or year tests; public examinations levels; marks at the bottom of pieces of homework. For many students, this approach is demoralizing and frustrating and contributes to the underachievement of some with the potential for high performance because:

1. They do not always understand how they can improve their work. A 'B – Good' tells an able student that the work is not worth an 'A' but not why.
2. They are not made aware of the standards they should be aiming for.
3. There are no pointers for a way forward.
4. They have had no involvement in the process, no opportunity to explain their reasoning or to debate the pros and cons of an idea.

> 'In English I was told that it would be a struggle for me to take the exams and now it's my subject at Cambridge. I used to be marked B and oceans of red all over my essays; it really discouraged me, so much that I started out doing Sciences. Then when I changed schools and had a teacher who used to rave about my essays, I thrived on his encouragement. It's probably a hangover that I still think it's terrible to think highly of your abilities.'
> Gifted student quoted in Freeman (2001:140)

One the other hand, assessment *for* learning is all about using assessment as part of the learning process and, importantly, involving students in the assessment process. Schools that aspire to excellent provision for their most able pupils will need to have a consistent school-wide approach to assessment for learning, to view it as part of effective planning at all levels and to regard it is an essential professional skill for all teaching and support staff.

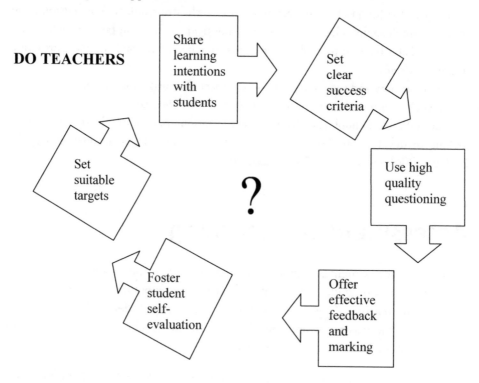

Key Elements of Assessment for Learning

Links with Parents and the Wider Community

Parents

The relationships forged between a school, parents, carers and the wider community impact on its ability to draw out students' gifts and talents. We have to be thankful that the days of the yellow line across a playground, over which parents were not expected to cross, are over but there is still a reluctance to involve parents in issues concerning the gifted and talented, especially in affluent communities.

Parents at all stages of compulsory education can:

- tell teachers about out-of-school interests and passions
- explain factors, both within the school and beyond, contributing to underperformance
- help children with homework and research
- support teachers in the personalization agenda and by helping with Individual Education Plans (IEP) when they are considered necessary
- contribute their own skills and expertise to the school by giving expert talks, becoming mentors, working alongside teachers
- suggest outside organizations that could help the school with its gifted and talented agenda.

There are some concerns that crop up over and over again from the parents of gifted and talented students:

- s/he is bored
- s/he needs to be moved up a year
- s/he will not do homework
- my child should not waste time on the subjects s/he's no good at
- s/he's badly behaved because s/he is gifted
- s/he is isolated
- s/he wants to be like her/his friends and they do not work.

Whether schools agree with the parents or not, it is important that parents' concerns are treated with respect and that all parties work together to resolve any difficulties so that children do not underachieve.

Schools and Colleges

Good relationships with other schools and colleges:

1. Contribute to smooth transition from one school to another so that able students do not have to re-prove their ability e.g. through bridging projects; gifted and talented summer schools; exchange teaching across key stages; planning for curricular progression across schools.
2. Allow schools to call on expertise within another school/college when they are finding it difficult to meet gifted or talented students' needs e.g. some primary schools arrange for teachers from local secondary schools to help them with pupils who have outstanding mathematical ability; increasingly FE colleges are contributing to the 14–19 curriculum for students whose abilities lie in drama, music or catering or where these colleges offer languages and other specialist courses that a school may not be able to put on; older pupils at primary or secondary level often work with gifted or talented pupils at an earlier key stage; partnerships between state and private schools are allowing able students from deprived areas to access teaching expertise within the private sector; Independent/State School Partnerships have been actively encouraged with funding available through the Building Bridges project. (Teachernet 2007)

Working with external agencies opens up a huge range of opportunities for the most able students and helps to make the school curriculum more varied and relevant.

Opportunities afforded by Workforce Remodelling and Dedicated PPA

The traditional set-up of one room, one teacher and 30 pupils of different abilities and inclinations made it very difficult to plan and implement a programme of work that catered for all those children, especially the most able. Workforce remodelling has created more support within the classroom for teachers and an increasingly ambitious body of teaching assistants is actively seeking a part in the delivery of lessons rather than just photocopying or hearing the slow readers. In these situations, and it has to be admitted that schools are only just beginning to get to grips with this model of working, there are many more opportunities for small group work with the most able. Some schools have also found that the act of providing adequate PPA (Planning, Preparation and Assessment) time for their teachers has had unexpected benefits for all pupils and in some cases for their gifted and talented students.

Case Study

This is a much-shortened version of a case study that appears at http://www.tda.gov.uk/case_studies/remodelling/bigfoot.aspx?keywords=bigfoot

Bigfoot Theatre in Education (TiE) company works across the London boroughs, Birmingham and Brighton, providing workshops, special drama projects and holiday courses.

The company also operates a supply service offering specialist drama practitioners as an alternative to traditional supply agencies. The success of this provision led some schools to engage Bigfoot to release PPA time for teachers on a regular basis.

Albion Primary School in Southwark is one of Bigfoot's customers. Albion has established the major part of its PPA release time with Bigfoot. Each year group at the school has a weekly half-day session with the Bigfoot tutor. All staff are very impressed by the quality of delivery. The drama sessions create an entirely positive buzz inside the school and 'fantastic' is the adjective most commonly ascribed to the provision.

Characteristics of the strategy to use Bigfoot theatre company to release PPA time at Albion school include:

→ continued...

- the Bigfoot sessions have chiefly focused on history and literacy curriculum areas
- the sessions also form an important part of the focus on speaking and listening skills identified in the School Improvement Plan
- the Bigfoot tutor plans sessions to complement curriculum areas which pupils are working on with class teachers
- there is no planning burden on teachers for the drama sessions
- teaching assistants at the school support the work of the Bigfoot tutors in the sessions
- the tutor reports to class teachers on pupils' progress.

The school intends to collaborate with Bigfoot on a long-term basis.

Although all children are benefiting from the Bigfoot experience, those with ability in drama must be revelling in this opportunity to work with experts in the field and develop their talent.

Another way in which PPA is having knock-on benefits for the most able is that, with more time to work on improving their assessment and monitoring techniques, teachers are beginning to recognize when their most able pupils are not being challenged and are finding ways of dealing with the problem.

Case Study

Again this is a very shortened version of a case study from http://www.tda.gov.uk/remodelling/nationalagreement/resources/casestudies/remodelling/st_peters.aspx

St Peter's Church of England (aided) Primary School is a small school with 198 pupils, located in Ashton-under-Lyne. The school has used cover supervision to release core subject leaders for monitoring and feedback. 'Through the monitoring we discovered that many teachers weren't stretching their gifted and talented children – we were able to take action in the space of one half-term, whereas without cover supervision it could have taken much longer to identify it.'

Many schools are now arranging CPD on gifted and talented education for their teaching assistants so that they understand the philosophy behind the English Model, as Deborah Eyre calls our provision for these pupils, and can be proactive in supporting teachers and pupils. (Eyre 2004:4)

4 Providing for Gifted and Talented Students at Classroom Level

General Aspects of Provision

Milly (Year 1) is lively and sociable with a wide general knowledge. She always takes the lead in discussion and group work, but she has no interest in reading and writing and her progress in these areas is comparatively slow.

Amy (Year 3) is in a class where the general level of achievement is low. Her poetry and narrative writing amaze her teachers while her mathematics and understanding of science put her on a par with children in Year 5. Her parents believe she needs access to children like herself.

Tom (Year 6) loves mathematics and is working at such a high level that a sixth former from the local secondary school is mentoring him. He reads and writes well although he shows little interest in books unless they are about mathematics. He does not find it easy to mix and squirms with embarrassment if asked to take part in drama sessions or work in groups.

Chloe (Year 9) excels in the classroom and on the sports field. She cannot decide what subjects to opt for next year because she has so many choices. Outside school she has a hectic social life and is a member of the local youth orchestra.

George (Year 11) is determined to be an actor. His out-of-school commitments, including some filming, often disrupt his schoolwork. The only time he shows any commitment to the school is when he is taking a leading role in a school production. GCSEs seem irrelevant to both him and his parents.

Although achieving at a steady level throughout his school career, Harry (Year 12) did not catch his teachers' attention until he entered sixth form and became involved in Young Enterprise activities. It soon became obvious that he was a natural entrepreneur and leader.

From the examples given above it is clear that schools cannot adopt a one-size-fits-all approach when providing for their most able students. Some want a competitive climate whilst others wither in such an environment. A few are very able across the curriculum but others excel in only one area. Some are sociable and love to work in groups and others are happy working on their own. Personalization of the curriculum is essential if all their various needs are to be met.

What is to be taught in the UK is set out in the National Curriculum, but it is *how* the curriculum is delivered that determines whether or not the most able (and others) are engaged and enthused.

> What we do know is that boredom and lack of cognitive challenge in the daily curriculum is playing a more significant role in causing pupils across the ability range to become disaffected than was originally suspected. Where there is pressure for so-called academic standards, to the exclusion of a concern for individuals and their needs (Hargreaves, 1984, Galloway and Goodwin, 1987) then this will predispose many children to feel alienated from school work. (Montgomery 2000:130)

Society needs a highly able and creative workforce, capable of problem-solving, cooperative working, communicating effectively in a variety of ways, self-organizing and able to learn from experience. Teaching needs to reflect these challenges.

At classroom level, all able children need:

- empathetic teachers
- an environment in which it is safe to be highly able
- their abilities to be recognized and provided for
- a wide variety of approaches to learning and teaching
- to be engaged by their learning
- to be challenged, sometimes to the point of failure
- opportunities to work with others like themselves
- opportunities to enrich and extend their learning
- access to a wide range of appropriate resources, including ICT
- access to experts
- effective and varied assessment for learning.

Classroom Environment

The learning of many gifted and talented students is very similar to that of a roller-coaster with rapid achievement one year followed by a period of uphill struggle or even stagnation the following when there is a change of teacher or school. Very often the key to the periods of rapid progress is a positive classroom climate – a climate that celebrates achievement at all levels, in which teachers and pupils learn alongside each other, where there is an atmosphere of mutual respect and individuality is prized, not discouraged.

Highly able students can be demanding, especially if they interrupt the flow of the lesson with constant questioning (which the teacher may be unable to answer), keep coming up with off-the-wall responses or work very quickly and demand attention. It is important to resist the urge to put such students firmly in their place or to convey exasperation to the rest of the class. Where able pupils are put down, they quickly learn to keep a lower profile. Some will start to underachieve because to do so is less exposing than allowing enthusiasms to put them at risk of mockery. This does not mean, of course, that able students should be allowed to get away with discourtesy or hogging all the teacher's time but problems should be dealt with quietly when other pupils are not around.

Ground rules need to be set in classrooms so that all abilities can flourish and criticism is constructive. This can be done by:

1. Teaching children to say, 'I think that would have been better if you had . . .' rather than 'I don't like that'. This helps to create a climate in which everyone can contribute and learn from the opinions of others.
2. Making it clear that teasing and bullying students because of their high ability is unacceptable.
3. Being sensitive to those pupils who feel exposed by public reward. Where a student, rightly or wrongly, believes that public recognition of their abilities will lead to unwanted attention from classroom bullies or will damage their credibility, a quiet word of praise or even a letter home to parents will be appreciated by the student where calling them to the front of the class or awarding them a certificate would not.
4. Saying to an able child who wants to answer all the questions, 'I'd like you to think about . . . and I'll come back to you later to hear your answer,' acknowledges their enthusiasm and gives others a chance to take part.
5. Modelling researching answers when the teacher is unable to answer questions or a topic takes the class in an unexpected direction. Students should also be helped to do this research themselves so that a community of enquiry is established. Able students appreciate honesty in their teachers and are quick to spot those who are creating a smoke screen rather than admitting their limitations.
6. Approaching the curriculum in a flexible manner so that, for example, able readers in Year 2 are not denied the reading books set aside for Years 3–6 if that is what they need.
7. Sometimes allowing students to negotiate how they approach or present a piece of work.
8. Making sure that quiet members of the class are rewarded for their efforts.

One concern often expressed by the parents of able girls is that they rarely receive reward and recognition for their efforts. Some recent work by the dcsf (2007:4–5,12–13) on able children who fail to make the expected level of progress between the end of KS1 and the end of KS2, has highlighted the problem of overlooked able children. Characteristics shared by many of these children are that:

- they are well-behaved
- they are 'easy to miss', often being undemanding and quiet
- they do not ask for help and find it difficult to identify their own successes
- in mathematics, they are often girls.

Case Study

Isabella (age 5) settled straight into school, coped easily with the work and gave the teacher no cause for concern. She didn't need to ask for help and bring herself to the attention of the teacher. The class teacher had told Isabella's parents that she was working very comfortably in the most able group in the class. Every Friday Isabella wept when she came out of school because she had not received a certificate in assembly. Before she had been in school for one term, she had noticed that these coveted certificates went either to the naughty boys who had managed to behave themselves for a while, or to more assertive able boys. Her mother could not decide whether to tell the school or wait for Isabella's efforts to be recognized. She was really worried that her daughter would stop trying.

Teachers

Clark (1995) found that teachers who appeared to be good at facilitating learning for the most able:

- were personable and treated learners with respect and as partners in the learning experience
- actively and routinely encouraged discussions of higher order thinking
- used time flexibly and scheduled or rescheduled as far as possible according to learner needs
- would, as far as possible, follow up independent study interests of students
- displayed traits of gifted behaviour; for example, they were heavily involved in many activities, both personally and professionally.

Many would add to that list 'had an excellent sense of humour' because this is a characteristic that appears to be particularly important to boys, as in the example below. Key words about the teacher's approach are in italics.

The best teacher I ever had was Mr. Tidyman in fifth grade. . . . He had an excellent *sense of humor*, told us *jokes and funny stories* all the time and *encouraged* us to be *free spirits*. He made school tremendous *fun*. He *taught us a ton* of math; more math than I learned in all three years of middle school combined. While kids in the other fifth grade classes were struggling with their multiplication tables, he made basic algebra and geometry *interesting* and commonsensical for us. This is how he taught us what reciprocal fractions are:

First of all, he asked if any of us already knew what the word "reciprocal" meant. None of us did, so he gave us a *demonstration*. He told this kid, Tony Gonzalez, to stand on a chair in front of the class. Tony was wary, but complied. When he had Tony satisfactorily situated upon the chair, Mr. T. motioned to him and said, "This is Tony." Then he said, "Ready?" Tony looked sideways at him and said something like, "Uh–" as Mr. Tidyman picked him up and turned him upside down. "This is the reciprocal of Tony," said Mr. Tidyman as he held the boy upside down about 3 feet above the ground. We all thought it was *funny as hell*. Tony turned beet red, but he thought it was funny too. Fractions were always a breeze.

Mr. T. *also loved* literature. He *read to us from Poe, Twain, Carroll*, etc. He taught us what stuff like *alliteration*, *metaphor* and *iambic pentameter* were and gave us *kickass* spelling words. Our very first spelling words on the very first day of school were *prognosticate* and procrastinate. Some of the stuff he had us read: Flowers for Algernon, Casey at the Bat, The Cremation of Sam McGee, Jabberwocky (*He had us memorize this. I still know it by heart*), The Secret of NIMH, The Raven, The Walrus and the Carpenter, The Celebrated Jumping Frog of Calaveras County. *He had us make up our own stories and read them aloud every week.* After each student read their story, there was *constructive criticism* from the class. *With an emphasis on the constructive part. Badmouthing fellow students was so not tolerated. He was very adamant about treating others with respect.*
(Everything 2000)

Obviously in the current climate, when physical contact with children is actively discouraged, it is probably not a good idea to turn children upside down! Nonetheless, what comes through from the description above is:

- the teacher's passion for learning
- his quirkiness
- his humour
- his HIGH EXPECTATIONS
- his knowledge.

Realistically, even the best of teachers will not stimulate high performance from all children. The teacher described earlier may well have frightened girls and younger pupils out of their minds. A superb teacher of English may turn herself inside out and never get a response from the pupil whose abilities profile is so lopsided that he has no interest whatsoever in literature and language. The gifted male Year 5 teacher may make no headway whatsoever with an able girl whose early experiences have taught her not to trust men. What we have to cultivate is a learning environment in which not only is it safe for gifted and talented students to achieve but it is equally safe for teachers to seek help, without losing face, when they cannot get through to a student or to assert their high assessment of a students' abilities where this has not been recognized by others.

Case Study

Jason in Year 4 was surly and uncooperative with his new young female teacher. His school career to date had been very patchy with tantrums and fighting in the infant classes and open hostility to his Year 2 teacher. In Year 3, the school thought that they had made a breakthrough. His behaviour and attitude changed dramatically and he was working with the most able group much of the time. In view of his regression in Year 4, the headteacher spoke to Jason's foster mother and found out that he had been distrustful of women ever since his mother walked out and he had had to go into care. In Year 3 he had established a strong relationship with his male teacher – hence the good progress. It was agreed that although Jason would stay with his new female teacher, his former teacher would mentor him on a weekly basis. This was not an overnight success but he grudgingly began to settle down and work again, knowing that he would have to show his work every week to his mentor.

Accounting for Prior Knowledge

When planning a unit of work, it is essential to account for students' prior knowledge of the topic. Able students often underachieve because the teacher or teachers are unaware of just what they can do. Problems at transition from one school to another have already been mentioned but the problems can also occur when children move from one class to another within a school because, even though a lot of informal chat takes place in staffrooms about children's abilities, this is not always formally recorded. Children then have to prove themselves all over again. Even the class teacher in primary school, who knows her pupils well, may not be aware of the amount of learning that has gone on outside school in the home, in clubs, in the community and beyond.

When trying to assess what children already know, teachers can turn to the obvious sources such as:

- SATs and other assessments
- Foundation Stage Profiles for reception teachers and KS1 teachers
- information from feeder schools

- other teachers
- reference to earlier KS materials (it is amazing how rarely this happens).

Within their own classrooms there are a number of additional strategies they can use including:

- *Brainstorming* – at the end of a lesson, spend five minutes brainstorming what pupils already know about the next topic. If it turns out that the most able know much more than was expected, planning will need to be modified so that these children are moving forward with their learning.
- *Pre-tests and homework tasks* – again these should be carried out before the introduction of the new topic. The homework tasks may be very simple, like making lists of everything they know about volcanoes; writing down words and places they associate with the Industrial Revolution; preparing a one minute talk on anything they know about the topic to be studied; giving them three or four graded examples of the next maths topic and asking if they can do any of them. Those familiar with the topic should just do the hardest example they can manage. This overcomes the problem of the most able being given more work than anyone else. These relatively simple measures will help to make sure that the teacher is ready for those pupils who will need work of a different quality.
- *Assessment built into early stages of module* – (see the Core Enhancement model later in this chapter).
- *Listening* – to what pupils say.
- *Using a picture as a trigger* – this can be used with any age group but is particularly useful with infant children. For example, many first schools arrange for groups to walk round the locality as part of their geography studies. Showing an old picture of the area and discussing changes that have taken place will alert teachers to those who are already very well-informed and might need more challenging tasks or more detailed information about some features.
- *Designing a quiz or computer game* – based on what they already know about a topic.
- *Creating a mindmap* – of what they currently know.

Curriculum Compacting

Having established what children already know, the curriculum can be compacted at classroom level for those who are well ahead of their peers by cutting out all unnecessary drill and practice of skills already mastered. Then pupils can be moved on to the next stage of learning (*extension*), which might involve looking at the curriculum for the next year group, or *enriching* the curriculum by:

- introducing books, topics or material not usually included in the curriculum; this is easy to do in subjects such as English, history, geography, RE and science
- approaching a topic from a totally different angle or adopting a problem solving approach
- carrying out a piece of research based on the work other pupils are doing
- studying another subject within a subject area e.g. some very able pupils study astronomy in addition to separate sciences.

Planning for the Full Ability Range

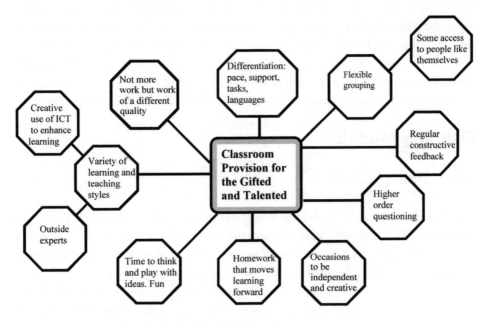

Classroom Provision for the Gifted and Talented

It is tempting to think that the problem of providing for our most able students could be resolved by simply setting pupils at every stage of schooling. Then differentiation would be unnecessary because teachers would be planning for an homogeneous group. What is often overlooked when this argument is made is that the biggest ability range is likely to be in the top set. This is particularly apparent in subjects like mathematics and modern foreign languages where there will be quite able steady workers as well as those whose natural affinity for the subject means that they may be way ahead of the teacher. In mathematics this can be just as true at the primary stage as at the secondary stage and very much more alarming for the class teacher who is not a maths specialist. To provide the same educational diet for the able plodders as for the instinctive mathematicians, linguists or scientists results in a gross disservice to both groups. Differentiation remains essential whether there is setting or not.

Planning for appropriate:

- pace
- depth
- breadth
- independence
- reflection

for the most able in the context of a mixed ability group or a setted group can be tackled in a number of ways. The approach will depend to some extent on the age of pupils, the subject and the personality and experience of the teacher. Some teachers, especially when they are beginning to think seriously about the most able for the first time, find it useful to use a planning model. For this reason, two have been included here. Whichever model is used (or not used) it is always best to plan for slightly above the level of learning you would normally expect to cover with a similar group. If teachers expect more, students often rise to the challenge and surprise them.

Planning Models

Must Should Could

The *Must Should Could* model was employed in much of the documentation from the former DfES. Basically, material, activities and concepts that *must* be covered by everyone in a class appear in the *must* section. This section represents the bottom line. If pre-testing has shown that some pupils have already grasped everything in the must section then they miss it out. The *should* section contains that which the majority of pupils should aspire to. Again, if pre-testing or conversation with able pupils show that they are comfortable with this section they move on to material in the *could* section. This will not be more of the same but will demand a higher level of thinking, more creativity or more demanding research. The strength of this approach is that if it is used well and teachers do take prior knowledge into account when deciding which level individual children will be working at, then different students will be working at the most advanced level for different topics. The gifted and talented group within the class will not (and should not) be set in stone.

Year 7 Introductory Lesson on Using a Bunsen Burner		
MUST *Absolutely necessary*	**SHOULD** *Desirable for whole class*	**COULD** *More open activity*
Follow the instructions for setting up, lighting and changing the Bunsen flame.	Understand how the flame changes and find a way of testing which flame was hottest.	Examine the reasons for the Bunsen burner design. Decide when it would be appropriate to use the different flames. Find other uses for the different flames.

Adapted from Alderman (2008:24)

Core Plus Enhancement

Another common approach often called **Core Plus Enhancement** has assessment built into the earliest stages (see the following figure). All pupils are given a core task or activity followed by a task assessment. On the basis of this, the majority of the class will continue with the core task whilst the higher achievers will move on to the enhanced task. An advantage of fitting assessment into the early stages is that the teacher does not start the lesson or unit with a preconceived idea of who should be capable of moving on to the enhanced work. The decision is based on how students respond to the initial core task.

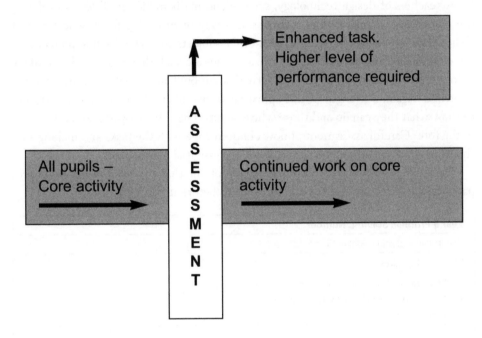

Core Plus Enhancement

The following table contains examples of core and enhanced activities used by KS2 teachers of English in Cheshire schools.

Core and Enhanced Activities used by KS2 Teachers	
1. Core Task **Able Children**	• Investigate formal language to create a passport • Use formal language to write a letter about something amusing
2. Core Task **Able Children**	• Fantasy genre – *Grimstone's Ghost* • Sentence level work – variety of sentence structures • Impersonate the sentence style of the fantasy genre to develop complex sentences

3. Core Task Able Children	• Investigating myths, legends and fables • Write own versions of myths, legends and fables • Write a dual purpose version adapting the language for a different audience: older reader–young reader
4. Core Task Able Children	• Poem 'Warning' by Jenny Joseph. Study as a class and use as a model for their own writing • Read the more complex poem 'Notes for the Future' and use as a model. Continue exploring the theme of old age by studying 'Café Portraits' and 'Home' by Paul Donnelly

Low Threshold/High Ceiling

Many teachers of design technology, science and mathematics at all levels prefer to use low threshold/high ceiling activities as a way of providing for a wide range of ability. The approach can be used with other subjects too. The starting point is the same for all children in the class but the activities are such that higher order thinking is fostered and additional extension activities are built in so that the most able are stretched. Again, a strength of this approach is that all children have an opportunity to show what they can do and those whose abilities have been overlooked may come to the fore. Careful assessment of how children cope with the tasks and making sure that they explain and evaluate their work are essential components.

The example below is a shortened version of one that appeared in the Resources pages of the gifted and talented Wise website before it was closed down.

Year 6 Problem Solving: Number
Unit 1: Generalizing – Make 23
Learning Objectives • Make general statements about odd or even numbers • Make and investigate a general statement • Explain reasoning
Introduction Ask pupils to imagine they have three bags full of numbers • The first is full of 1s • The second is full of 3s • The third is full of 5s Ask them to take out four numbers from any bags (e.g. 1,1,1,5) and add them together. Can they make a total of 12 from the four numbers? How many different ways of doing this are there?
Main Activities Using the same three bags of imaginary numbers still containing 1s, 3s, and 5s, pupils are asked to take out six numbers and make the target sum of 23. After two minutes they share solutions with a partner, asking their partner to check their arithmetic. Ask the following questions: • What numbers can you make? • Have you kept a record of the totals made?

- What do you notice about your totals?
- What can you say about these types of numbers?
- Can you make 23 with a different number of numbers? How many?
- Can you explain why?
- How do you know two odd numbers added together make an even?
- Can you convince us all of your conclusion?

Plenary
Discuss the explanations. Which did you prefer? Can you change the problem so that it would work? Ask a similar question using a different number of bags or different numbers in the bags.

Extension Activity
Investigate the sums of any two or three consecutive numbers. What do you notice? Can you make some statements you think are always true? Can you justify your findings? How about sums of more than three consecutive numbers?

While pupils are working on the initial task, teachers must circulate amongst groups and individuals getting them to explain their reasoning, actively encouraging them to move on to the next stage and being ready to step in when it is obvious that the extension activity is required.

Flexible Grouping

Flexible grouping within the classroom is another way of providing challenge for the most able. There will be occasions when putting what are perceived to be the most able pupils together in one group is appropriate because everyone needs time to be with others like themselves. But there will be other times when groups should be designed to contain a range of abilities and skills with every student taking on a different role.

Expert Groups

Another approach is to establish an expert group, who receive instruction on an aspect of a topic from a teacher while the rest of the class is supervised by a teaching assistant or getting on with some other work. Alternatively, the expert groups can be sent off to research something on the computer or in the library/resource centre. Afterwards an expert joins each group within the class and passes on what they have learnt. The experts have to sort out what they have learnt in their heads so that they can communicate it clearly. This is a very effective strategy because there is abundant evidence that the best way to learn and understand something is to teach it (see the following figure). The recipients of the information usually enjoy this activity too and are more confident about asking questions from a peer than they might be from a teacher. Subjects such as English, RE, history and geography lend themselves to this approach in all key stages.

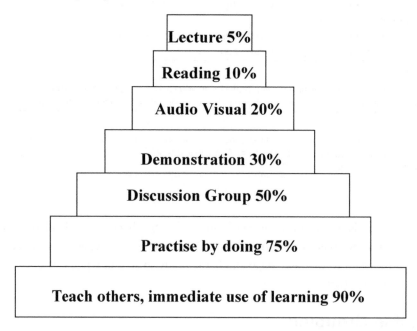

Methods of Information Delivery and Retention Rates

Learning as a Social Activity

Although there will be many times when it is appropriate for able students to work on their own, it is essential that they get regular support and feedback. Teachers, parents and other adults play a crucial part in helping them to reach their potential because, according to Lev Vygotsky, learning is most effective when it is part of a social interaction with a 'More Knowledgeable Other'. He called the difference between what students can achieve on their own and what they can achieve with the support of a more experienced person, in whatever field is being studied, the Zone of Proximal Development. (Simplypsychology 2008) For example, an able 7-year-old, sent off to research a topic in the school library, may come across unfamiliar language that makes it difficult for him/her to make any progress. If there is an adult who can interpret that language, learning can then move forward. A young musician, having difficulty playing a piece of music because his/her technique is faulty, is unlikely to become a better musician unless the faulty technique is identified and corrected by a more experienced musician. Sometimes a More Knowledgeable Other (MKO) simply needs to ask a few questions to set the learner on the right track; on other occasions instruction, demonstration or explanation will be necessary. MKOs may also be peers, older students, e-mentors or outside experts.

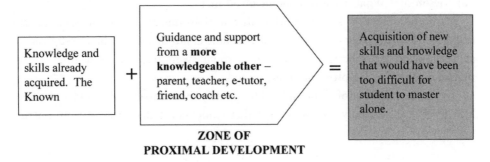

ZONE OF PROXIMAL DEVELOPMENT

Zone of Proximal Development

Ferretti (2007:115) describes an excellent geography activity for Year 7 pupils, which could easily be adapted for older or younger students. They are asked to imagine that they are travelling from the North Pole to the South Pole. They have to choose a line of longitude along which to travel so that they pass through at least five countries. They research the five countries and then write about what they saw, who they met and describe the adventures they had. This writing can be in the form of a diary, a set of emails, postcards from each country or a tape recording of their travels.

This is an activity that many very able students would really relish but there is a danger that it could become a cut and paste exercise unless there is an MKO who is posing well placed and challenging questions and directing them to appropriate resources. Question: Why is country A so rich and country B so poor? With appropriate support this will get them to consider climate, history, governance, resources, fair trade, transport, disease and many other factors rather than simply producing descriptive material.

Questioning and Higher Order Thinking

Questioning

Much is currently written about the importance of teachers' questioning skills in raising attainment in the classroom. Research by Kerry (reported in Wallace 1992:61) showed that about 21 per cent of the questions asked in primary classrooms were about classroom management (Have you got a pencil?) and only 3.5 per cent required children to use higher order thinking skills. The other 75.5 per cent were simple questions designed to find out if information had been received (When did Nelson die? What battle was he involved in?).

A common practice is that of firing off questions quickly and demanding instant responses. What usually happens is that the same children answer the questions over and over again and others, who may know the answers but like more time to formulate a response, are often underestimated.

To get the most out of all pupils and to identify those capable of thinking at a very high level, it is generally recommended that students are discouraged from putting up their hands and that:

1. They are given more time to respond to questions. This usually means they come up with more detailed and considered responses.
2. Some questions are 'planted' with an individual pupil or group of pupils for a while before the teacher returns to them to check their responses.
3. Questioning is more targeted so that all pupils are involved in the lesson and cannot daydream while others work. It also allows the teacher to direct more demanding questions to the most able.
4. Unusual responses are encouraged and handled with sensitivity.
5. Initial responses are followed up with secondary more probing questions as in these from Brown et al. (1993:21)
   ○ Does that always apply?
   ○ Can you give me an example of that?
   ○ How does that fit in (relevance)?
   ○ You say it is X, what particular kind of X?
   ○ What are the exceptions?
   ○ Why do you think that is true?
   ○ Is there another view?
   ○ What is the idea behind that?
   ○ Can you tell me the difference between the two?
6. 'What if' questions are used to inspire debate and controversy. Hunt (2007:86) gives examples of 'what if' questions that can be used in RE. What if euthanasia was available on demand for everyone over the age of 80? What if all RE in schools was abolished? What if an angel appeared to you while you were alone in the middle of the night?

Thinkers' Keys

Braggett (1997:231) summarizes T. Ryan's approach to helping students become effective and flexible thinkers. Ryan has developed a set of 20 distinct approaches to teacher questioning.

1. **The Reverse Key:**
   Use: never, could not, etc.

2. **Consequence Key:**
   What would be the consequence if . . .
3. **The Disadvantage Key:**
   List disadvantages of . . . Correct, eliminate, modify parts.
4. **The Combination Key:**
   List attributes of two dissimilar objects. Find ways to combine them.
5. **The BAR Key:**
   Make something bigger, add something, replace something.
6. **The Alphabet Key:**
   Find related topic words for every letter of the alphabet.
7. **The Variation Key:**
   How many ways can you . . .
8. **The Picture Key:**
   How does this picture link to the topic?
9. **The Prediction Key:**
   Predict what would happen if . . .
10. **The Different Uses Key:**
    Find ten or more uses for . . .
11. **The Ridiculous Key:**
    Make a ridiculous statement and then justify it.
12. **The Commonality Key:**
    Find common elements between two unrelated objects.
13. **The Questions Key:**
    Start with an answer. What was the question?
14. **The Brainstorming Key:**
    Use *How to* . . . starters.
15. **The Invention Key:**
    Plan or make something unique.
16. **The Brick Wall Key:**
    State the impossible and then suggest ways around it.
17. **The Construction Key:**
    Use a plan/do/check strategy to construct using simple materials.
18. **The Forced Relationship Key:**
    Problem solving using dissimilar objects.
19. **The Alternative Key:**
    Complete tasks using unusual strategies.
20. **The Interpretation Key:**
    Describe an unusual situation and explain why it is happening.

It is just as important that students are encouraged to *ask* probing questions about their work. Susskind (1969) in the United States found that most teachers asked questions at the rate of two a minute but that pupils asked on average two per hour and many of these were not to do with the subject under discussion. It would be interesting to know if the situation is the same in the United Kingdom now.

Hotseating

Hotseating can be used at any phase and in any subject to get students involved and to encourage them to ask searching questions. There are many variations but a good starting point is for the teacher to sit in the hot seat. In early years classes, s/he might be a character from a nursery rhyme, in history s/he might be an historical character at a crucial stage in his/her life, in art s/he could be Picasso, in science someone who made a dramatic breakthrough. The possibilities are limitless. The teacher will need to have modelled good questioning. Once this has been done, students are invited to ask questions in order to get a better understanding of the person. As students become more confident and familiar with the process they can begin to assume the hot seat.

History Hotseating

Whilst interviewing a single character can be great fun, a whole extra dimension is added by making the interview a "head to head" between two characters with opposing opinions. One of my favourite Year 8 lessons involves presenting myself as Martin Luther and giving deliberately provocative but substantiated responses to a series of pre-prepared questions ("Do you think that the Bible should be in Latin?", "Are pilgrimages important?"). Storming out at the end of the interview, I then return as Pope Leo X to answer exactly the same questions from the opposite viewpoint. In the follow-up lesson, students explain which point of view they found most convincing and consider what the speakers agreed about (issues of fact) despite their obvious differences (issues of opinion). Biased newspaper reports can then be produced in favour of their candidate ("Luther wisely argued . . . but the Pope stupidly raged that . . ."), complete with a suitably one-sided headline. More challenging still, get students to act as arbitrators, writing a verdict on the key issues which they hope will prove acceptable to both sides. This format can easily be adapted for any historical issue in which partisan viewpoints are the order of the day: the clash between Becket and Henry II, the Protestant-Catholic divide in Northern Ireland, the Arab-Israeli conflict in the Middle East. (Tarr 2003)

Higher Order Thinking

Bloom's Taxonomy

The fostering of higher order thinking and questioning is one of the keys to appropriate provision for our most able pupils. Many years ago Benjamin Bloom came up with a hierarchy of thinking skills, which has become known as Bloom's Taxonomy. The table below shows the taxonomy together with trigger words associated with questioning and classroom activities for each level of thinking. Teachers should regularly check lesson and unit plans to make sure that there are plenty of activities that, as a matter of course, require pupils to apply, analyse, synthesize and evaluate their knowledge.

Bloom's Taxonomy		
Level of Thinking		**Trigger words for questions and activities**
KNOWLEDGE (Low)	Observing and recalling information. Remembering something previously learned.	Tell; Recite; List; Locate
COMPREHENSION (Low)	Understanding information. Grasping meaning. Interpreting facts. Predicting consequences.	Explain; Outline; Show; Edit; Summarize; Describe
APPLICATION (Middle)	Using knowledge to solve problems.	Use; Illustrate; Make; Build; Demonstrate; Map; Calculate
ANALYSIS (High)	Seeing patterns. Understanding how parts relate to the whole. Recognizing structure.	Investigate; Classify; Compare; Contrast; Categorize; Separate
SYNTHESIS (High)	Use old ideas to create new ones. Generalize from given facts. Relate knowledge from different sources.	Design; Compose; Create; Hypothesize; Rearrange; Interpret; Imagine; Predict
EVALUATION (High)	Make judgements. Assess the value of something against a set of criteria. Compare and discriminate between ideas.	Judge; Recommend; Evaluate; Prioritize; Decide; Argue; Rate; Give opinions

One primary school in Warrington, regularly prepares activities using Bloom's Taxonomy to make sure that the most able pupils are catered for. The table below is one example.

FAIR TRADE FORTNIGHT	
Knowledge	List five different fair trade products.
	Locate five countries where Fair Trade products originate on a world map.
	Write a Fair Trade A to Z.
Comprehension	Prepare a flow chart to illustrate the journey from tea leaves to Fair Trade tea bags.
	Explain to a classmate what we mean by 'fair trade'.
	Make a cartoon strip describing a typical day in the tea fields.
Application	Keep a diary of your first day working in the tea fields.
	Prepare invitations for your fair trade tea party.
	Construct a flowchart to show how fair trade chocolate makes it into our shops.
	Design a new fair trade symbol.
	Plot the journey of a cup of fair trade tea from field to shop on a world map.
Analysis	Compare fair trade chocolate to other cheaper alternatives.
	Design a questionnaire to gather information about children's favourite chocolate bars.
	Prepare a report giving information about the different fair trade products on sale.
	Make a flow chart to show the critical stages in the making of fair trade chocolate.
Synthesis	Create a new fair trade product and plan a marketing campaign.
	Design a marketing poster for a new fair trade product.
	Develop a menu for a new fair trade restaurant using a variety of fair trade products.
	Invent a machine to grind fair trade coffee beans.
Evaluation	Why should people buy fair trade coffee and tea instead of cheaper alternatives?
	Write a letter to a tea plantation owner advising them on changes needed in the pay/working conditions of their company.
	Write a speech to persuade children in your class/school to buy fair trade products.
	Write a report to justify how much a packet of fair trade teabags should cost.

Philosophy for Children

Philosophy for Children (P4C), the brainchild of Matthew Lipman, aims to foster reasoning abilities and higher order thinking through a group philosophical approach. It can be used from KS1–KS4 and within many subjects, but it is most often used in the primary classroom and in RE lessons. Children sit in a circle so that they can see and be seen by everyone. A trigger, which could be a question a child wants to ask, a story or a picture, is used to start the session. The teacher must lay careful ground rules as far as listening to and having respect for each other are concerned. S/he then tries to establish a community of enquiry by asking children to respond to questions about the trigger. For example, if the original question was 'Is it always wrong to steal?' the teacher might then ask:

- Does anyone think it is always wrong to steal?
- Why is it wrong?
- What do you think would happen if you were to steal from a friend or your family?
- Should you steal from a stranger?
- What should happen to someone who steals?
- Does anyone disagree and think that it is not always wrong to steal?
- When would it not be wrong to steal?
- Can you give any more examples?

Obviously the teacher questioning would depend to a large extent on the responses she received from the children. The discussion might end with the teacher and children summarizing arguments put forward in the discussion and trying to draw them together into some sort of conclusion. In some cases, children may go away to research a topic further before coming together on another occasion to continue the discussion or take up another question related to the first. Although thinking aloud in a communal setting is beneficial to all children, the most able will be able to explore the issues at much greater depth and help to move the thinking of less able children forward.

As with all stand-alone thinking programmes, it is important that the approaches used in P4C sessions are incorporated into all lessons if they are to be effective. (Sapere 2008)

De Bono's CORT Thinking

Even gifted and talented students can find it difficult to sort out the thoughts they have floating around in their heads. CORT Thinking is a useful resource that provides a range of strategies for organizing ideas and material. For example, PMI stands for Plus, Minus, Interesting. When faced with a statement such as 'Oliver Cromwell was an evil man,' students put ideas or information that support that statement in the plus column, those that negate it in the minus column and anything that is neither a plus nor a minus but is nonetheless interesting in the interesting column. The ideas gathered can then be used in essay, classroom debate or any other presentation. Where a school adopts this kind of approach wholeheartedly it is likely to influence students' thinking ability. It is much less likely to have an impact if it is a one-off or weekly event that is not applied to ordinary classroom situations.

Proposal – All cars should be painted yellow		
Plus **(P)**	Minus **(M)**	Interesting **(I)**
• Cheaper if only one colour is on offer • Buying a car will be quicker • Fewer arguments between men and women • Very cheerful • Matching colour after an accident will be easier	• Boring • Too bright • Difficult to find your car in a car park • More difficult for police to track criminals • Colour attracts insects • People need to express personality through car colour	• What other methods would drivers use to personalize their cars? • How would you describe your car to someone else? • Would people introduce shades of yellow?

De Bono's Thinking Hats

Using De Bono's Thinking Hats encourages students to look at things from several different perspectives. It can be used in all schools and subjects (although more commonly in the humanities) and is increasingly used in business training courses. Some teachers place charts of Thinking Hats round the room to help discussion.

White	calls for information known or needed
Green	focuses on creativity, the possibilities and new ideas
Red	signifies feelings, hunches and intuition
Blue	is used to manage the thinking process
Yellow	symbolizes brightness and optimism
Black	is judgment – the devil's advocate or why something may not work

The following is an example of how Thinking Hats can be used to focus students' thinking. Although this is a secondary school activity, a similar approach could be used with older primary students.

Using De Bono's Thinking Hats in a Science, PSHE or RE Lesson

A previous homework task asks students to find out all they can about human–animal hybrid embryos so that they are able to answer the questions:

- What are scientists planning to do with human and animal embryos?
- Why?
- Who objects to this and why?

In the lesson, give six able students a piece of flipchart paper and a thick pen. Each of them is asked to write the name of their coloured hat at the top of the paper with a very brief explanation, for example, White Hat – Information, Red Hat – Emotions.

The teacher writes on the board: Scientists want to introduce animal material into human cells to help with research into some diseases.

S/he leads a discussion, first of all drawing from students the facts, not people's opinions. The White Hat student records the facts as they are provided.

If the scientists are successful, what are the likely benefits? Here the Yellow Hat student records the optimistic view of this research.

How might this research be developed in the future? Green Hat records these possibilities.

What are the dangers? These are recorded by Black Hat.

Who objects to this research? The feelings of Roman Catholics and other people should be recorded under the Red Hat together with the feelings of scientists whose work might be stopped and other interested parties (e.g. those suffering from incurable diseases).

When all the information and opinions have been gathered, the group tries to draw together some conclusions. The Blue Hat records these.

Assessing students' learning could be done in a number of ways:

1. The information gathered could be used as the basis for a formal debate.
2. Groups could be asked to produce two public information posters – one representing the views of researchers and one representing the views of an opponent or opponent group.
3. Students could use video recording equipment to create a televised debate between various interested parties such as the Roman Catholic Church, the researchers, charities representing people with incurable diseases.
4. PowerPoint presentations could be made by groups or individuals.
5. Students could carry out further research and present an extended piece of writing on the topic.
6. Mobile phones with videos could be used to interview people round the school and to record their attitudes to the topic.
7. Students could research attitudes in other countries and compare them with those in the UK.

Subject-Specific Thinking Materials

The publication of Leat's (1998) *Thinking Through Geography* for secondary schools spawned a host of imitations in other subjects and in the primary phase. Using these materials, students are required, among other things, to:

- Identify the odd one out. Hunt (2007:71) suggests using this activity in RE lessons. For example, the Roman Catholic Church: the Pope, priests, bishops. Which is the odd one out and why?
- Solve mysteries. Leat (1998:68–75) sets one mystery: 'In recent months, piglets and chickens have been disappearing from Loxley Coppice Farm – you have to decide why this has been happening.' This is preceded with considerable input on farming and then groups of students are given cards, each containing a separate piece of information. They have to decide which information they should discard and which to use to solve the mystery. Activities such as this can be modified for younger children.
- Identify fact or opinion.
- Retell stories. This is a good strategy for getting students to absorb and engage with information that can be quite dry if taught without an element of human interest. At the simplest level, a class is split into groups of three and the students given the numbers 1, 2 or 3 with the 1s being the most able pupils. Numbers 2 and 3 may be sent to the library or organized by a teaching assistant in some other task while the teacher reads a story with a human interest and containing key information (this may be in any subject) to the 1s. They listen carefully, ask questions and make notes. Then the 2s are invited in and the 1s retell the story and check their understanding. Lastly the 3s return and the 2s retell the story with the support of the 1s. There are more sophisticated versions for older students.
- Read photographs – Barnes (2007:83) uses the cartoon Peace and Future Cannon Fodder together with the questions: What does this source definitely tell me? What guesses can I make – what can I infer? What doesn't the source tell me? What other questions do I need to ask?
- Classify.

In all the above activities, students are expected to justify decisions and explain their reasoning. These approaches are particularly useful for able students who enjoy the challenge they present and the opportunities to explore ideas rather than simply being told facts.

> Thinking and talking about thinking is termed **metacognition**. It is through this process that pupils start to gain an insight into thinking and learning, and build up an explicit understanding of **major concepts in geography** which can be **transferred** to other contexts. (Leat 1998:2)

Creativity

Opportunities to display **creativity** are essential for all and particularly for those with the potential for high performance. But what is creativity?

A boy taking part in a school sand sculpture competition

'Creativity is the application of knowledge and skills in new ways to achieve a valued goal. To achieve this, learners must have four key qualities:

- the ability to identify new problems, rather than depending on others to define them
- the ability to transfer knowledge gained in one context to another in order to solve a problem
- a belief in learning as an incremental process, in which repeated attempts will eventually lead to success
- the capacity to focus attention in the pursuit of a goal, or set of goals.' (Seltzer et al. 1999:10)

Clear links can be seen in the definition above with Renzulli's Three-Ringed Conception of Giftedness and the Torrance Tests of Creative Thinking.

It is ironic that, at a time when the curriculum in England has become more and more prescriptive, countries like China are turning to us for guidance on nurturing creativity because they realize that a well-disciplined but blinkered and risk-averse workforce will not be able to meet the demands of the twenty-first century. Barriers to creative thinking include:

- lack of time
- content-heavy curriculum
- an exam structure that dominates pedagogy
- a rigid and unsupportive classroom atmosphere
- an unwillingness on the part of students to tackle challenges for fear of failure

These barriers must be recognized and tackled head-on if we are not to sleepwalk into producing children who can pass examinations but are frightened of offering an original suggestion.

Starter and plenary activities could include:

- working alone or in groups to generate mindmaps and spidergrams
- producing a list of questions that they hope will be answered in the course of the lesson
- coming up with alternative uses for ordinary classroom equipment
- making acrostics from key words for the lesson
- making up new words and definitions relating to the subject or topic
- putting previous learning into a song, poem or rap

Help to create a climate in which creativity will flourish.

Allowing students to vary the ways in which they respond to tasks and, where appropriate, encouraging unusual and even zany responses will further enhance a creative atmosphere. When subject barriers are crossed, whether in the primary or secondary school, opportunities for creative approaches to learning, that draw out unrecognized talent, abound.

Case Study

Innovative Graphics within Maths and Textile Design (A modified version of one by Holder 2007)

Students experimented with creating tessellations on a range of plotting papers with a focus on 90 degree rotations. They also created tessellations in response to the work of M. C. Escher which clearly identified repeated reflections and rotations.

Students transferred, enlarged and decreased the size of original sketchbook designs through CAD programs using worksheets. The scale of their designs was increased/decreased within a set layout of 20cm x 20cm. Students gained an understanding that transformations can be described as a series of reflections or rotations. Within textiles they learnt to increase and decrease the scale of drawings/designs using random scale appropriate to task.

Students were able to evaluate and question their own creative process and learning outcomes as they progressed using diaries, questionnaires, group/peer discussion/feedback and video footage. Students who had shown no interest in art suddenly found themselves being 'creative' and were thrilled at what they had produced. They showed a clear understanding of the maths behind their creations and the art within the maths. They were

→ continued ...

able to identify and explain the mathematical concepts (such as the properties of a tessellation) and at times surprised themselves with their knowledge!

Teachers were highly motivated by having developed a programme that was informative and progressive as well as being practical and enjoyable, but the planning and preparation needed to undertake a project of this kind was substantial.

Assessment for Learning (AfL)

There can be little doubt that AfL can be a major motivating force for getting able students to understand what stage they are at in their learning and what targets they need to set in order to move forward. The key elements of a school-wide AfL strategy were mentioned in Chapter 3. At classroom level, teachers will need to be aware of classroom dynamics and individual sensitivities among students if AfL is to be a positive experience for all.

Ainsworth (2007) described how he divided a group of very able pupils' exercise books into three piles, gave all the books in one pile a tick and a single word comment such as 'Good', gave all the books in the second pile a positive sentence complimenting them on some aspect of their work and wrote a formative comment on every book in the third pile explaining what to do to reach the next level. Afterwards pupils were invited to respond to the different marking strategies. The outcome was interesting in that 100 per cent found the single word comment a positive experience, 80 per cent found the encouraging sentence positive but only 60 per cent felt that formative comments were positive. This demonstrated all too clearly that teachers should exercise care in order to make formative assessment a motivating and rewarding experience. In our enthusiasm to help pupils progress with their learning we need to bear in mind that many feel threatened by what they perceive as criticism and will continue to need plenty of encouragement and praise. Assessment has an emotional impact which teachers should never ignore.

Peer-assessment, where pupils are evaluating a partner's work against a set of criteria, is a very valuable tool and will often provoke heated debate and analysis. It can also make able pupils aware of how differently people respond to the same task and help them to gain a better understanding of their own strengths and weaknesses. However, it is important to remember that this can also be a very intimidating experience especially if there is animosity between two pupils or one feels markedly inferior to the other. Teachers will need to lay very careful ground rules and model constructive criticism before this is attempted. They should also pair pupils sensitively and be on the lookout for any mocking or bullying. For a 'fragile' able student, such as a timid child or one who is a looked-after, particular care will need to be exercised. The learning targets set for such students may also need to be incrementally smaller as they tend to underestimate their abilities and are easily outfaced by what they consider to be overambitious next steps.

The traffic light system in which students give a piece of work they have completed a green if they found it easy, orange if there were areas of uncertainty and red if they found it very difficult is useful for all students but, for the most able, it will help to indicate those who are constantly getting green, possibly coasting and needing more challenge.

Asking the most able students to feedback on what they have learned to the rest of the class is another useful form of formative assessment.

There is an abundance of subject-specific material on AfL on the dcsf Standards website.

Learning Beyond the Classroom

Multiple Intelligences

Gardner (1993) believes he has empirical evidence of many different types of intelligence (see the following figure) and that awareness of an individual's intelligence profile can help the teacher and the individual to find successful ways of learning.

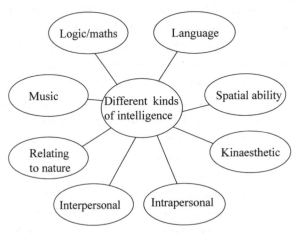

Gardner's Multiple Intelligences

The intelligences that students are most likely to be expected to use in the classroom are those described as linguistic and mathematical. These are also the ones on which IQ and many other standardized tests are based. For students who have strong interpersonal skills and want plenty of opportunity to interact with others, or those with high bodily-kinaesthetic ability who come to life when they are active, or the students with empathy for the natural world, traditional classroom teaching does not always allow them to demonstrate their true abilities. Although teachers are beginning to change their teaching methods to take account of these differences, it is outside the classroom where many of our able students get the experiences that enthuse them.

It is outside the classroom where many of our able students get the experiences that enthuse them

The 14–19 Strategy

The importance of learning beyond the conventional classroom has been acknowledged in the 14–19 Strategy. Secondary schools are now being encouraged to work in partnership with other schools with different specialisms, local businesses and colleges to provide a **personalized education** for young people. Although many able students will continue to do traditional A Levels, there are many others, equally able but different, who will not thrive in this academic environment. The 14–19 Strategy, through a wide range of practical courses – many of them work-based – will enable students to learn in entirely different ways in an adult environment. The Pathway trials carried out so far suggest that many able students, who were in danger of dropping out, have been re-enthused by this new approach to learning and have started to demonstrate really high levels of ability and to see the relevance of what they are being taught. There should also be opportunities for able students with particular specialisms to spend some school time in institutions where those specialisms can be developed. For example, if there is a particularly strong ICT programme in a local FE or an advanced music course in a different school/college, students should be able to access these.

The 14–19 Strategy is still in its infancy but if opportunities beyond the ordinary classroom are seen only as a way of supporting the less able, it will be a golden opportunity missed for many of our gifted and talented students.

Extended Day

After a few bleak years when extra-curricular activities all but disappeared in many schools, after-school clubs have reappeared, whether they are done under the auspices of an **extended day** programme or organized by enthusiastic teachers. It is almost impossible to overstate the importance of these activities to students. Young Engineer and science clubs encourage students to experiment and apply knowledge in ways that the classroom environment does not always allow. The school choir or orchestra brings together children from all over the school with similar interests. The maths club, whether at primary or secondary level, frees up the very able student who underplays his/her abilities in the classroom. The debating society brings out students who are interested in society and politics. For teachers who do not know how to get started in organizing such activities, there are plenty of organizations that will offer all kinds of support – experts, practical help, equipment, finance, certificates and other incentives. A few are listed in the back of this book.

Out-of-school clubs encourage students to experiment and apply knowledge in ways that the classroom environment does not always allow

Equally important are off-site visits, residential activities and work experience. The able child from a very supportive background may regularly makes trips abroad and visit places of interest but for those from homes where parents do not have the resources or the inclination to offer this kind of support, these activities assume a much more important role. Able children cannot fulfil their potential if:

- their parents have never worked and they do not understand the requirements and conventions of the working world
- they do not have access to computers and books at home (more of this in the next chapter) and the school does not offer this access through clubs and other activities
- they are uncomfortable in unfamiliar social settings
- they have never stayed away from home and been exposed to different patterns of behaviour
- they do not mix with adults and students from other social, ethnic and interest groups
- they never meet enthusiastic experts in a range of fields.

In England, all students aged from 4 to 19 who have been included in the PLASC school census return as gifted or talented should be signed up with the national Young, Gifted and Talented programme. This will give them access to day, weekend and holiday courses organized by their local regional Excellence Hub.

University and School Students Working Together at Liverpool University

General Tips for Engaging Able Students in the Classroom

1. Make sure that work for gifted and talented students differs in quality, not quantity – they should not have to do more work than others.
2. Avoid what Joan Freeman calls The Three Times Problem – explaining a task to the whole class, then again for those who were not listening and again just to be on the safe side – by which time many able students will have switched off. Direct additional explanations to those who need it and allow the most able to get on. (Freeman 2001:127)
3. Use personalized homework tasks to challenge students who need more stimulation or are nervous of working on different assignments in class. See Goodhew (2001) for some examples.
4. Keep a box of fun thinking puzzles in the corner of the primary classroom for students who finish very early. (Pupils will need some kind of feedback/interest from the teacher or they may not do them.)
5. Have a box of quick subject-specific thinking activities for use at the end of a lesson or when one group finishes before the rest. Some departments have graded activities to encourage students to stretch themselves by moving through the levels.
6. Build up a list of suitable websites for students wishing to research topics in greater depth. The school librarian may be able to help.
7. Use able students to record key points on the board during discussion sessions.
8. At the beginning of a lesson ask a group of able students to prepare the plenary session.
9. Where edited texts are used, give the most able students access to the full version.
10. Occasionally, limit the number of words able students can use to get across a particular idea. This forces them to use language very accurately.
11. Use students' gifts or talents in other areas to enhance classroom learning. For example, ask the creative lyricist to create a rap on a topic being covered in any subject or the keen design technology student to model a particular landform for geography.
12. Have fun.

5 Three Important Issues: Exceptional Ability (EA); Literacy; and ICT

Exceptionally Able Students

The exceptionally able (EA) – those students whose abilities in one or more fields are *far* in advance of their chronological age – have particular needs and present particular challenges for their teachers.

Emotional Development

One myth that needs to be scotched is that exceptionally able students are always social misfits and emotionally immature. Freeman (1998:27) reports that on the basis of her research and that of others: 'There is no reliable evidence to show that exceptionally high ability *per se* is associated with emotional problems.' She goes on to state: 'In fact, some studies of the gifted have indeed found them to be emotionally stronger than others, with higher productivity, higher motivation and drive, and lower levels of anxiety.'

Where emotional and social problems do occur it may be because:

1. Being labelled exceptionally able or gifted puts huge pressure on some students. Freeman (2001:195) comments on the differences between those labelled gifted and those of equal ability who were not labelled.
2. 'The idea that gifted children were bound to be "odd", and accordingly unhappy, circulated among parents and teachers, so that some looked for it and found it, and at times even seemed to encourage it. When a bright child was unhappy, it was often the gifts that got the blame. Yet there, in the same class as the labelled gifted, loaded with expectations, there were unlabelled others – of identical gifts who were neither expected to be nor were emotionally disturbed.'
3. Clearly there is food for thought here, given the current preoccupation with labelling.
4. Motor or other skills are not as well developed as their intellectual abilities, causing frustration. This is

often seen in younger exceptional students who are unable to express their complex ideas in writing because they lack the necessary manual dexterity.

5. Parents and teachers may expect the emotional and social development of such youngsters to be as advanced as their intellectual ability. Often in these respects, they simply are not. One 6-year-old, confidently coping with GCSE maths, nonetheless dealt with frustrations in the way many children of that age would do. For example, he found that he could always get attention by standing with his arms outstretched between the teacher and her class or any person she happened to be speaking to. The teacher did not expect that level of behaviour from a child with such advanced maths skills and regarded him as odd. It is important to remember that 6-year-old prodigies are still 6 years old.

6. There may be dual exceptionality (e.g. case study on page 109), where neither the exceptional ability nor the genuine difficulties (dyslexia in this case) are recognized, and a student becomes demotivated and resentful.

7. They are insufficiently challenged.

Supporting EA Students with Social or Emotional Problems

Despite the evidence of their balanced approach to life, many able students do admit that, though they appear confident and sociable, they are often 'alone in their heads' because there is no one with whom they can share the ideas and thoughts they have. Others do become isolated when they are 'prickly' towards their peers or even contemptuous of their relative lack of ability. Unfortunately, in a few cases, parents may reinforce these attitudes.

Schools can support isolated EA students in a number of ways:

1. Teachers need to take care that they do not (usually unintentionally) collude with children who mock the mannerisms and attitudes of EA students. A raised eyebrow, a laugh or a sigh from a teacher will tell students that it is acceptable to tease the child who provoked this reaction. (See case study on page 109.)

2. Anti-bullying policies should be acted on in relation to these students with the same vigour as they would be for racial discrimination.

3. In both primary and secondary schools, putting in place a SEAL (Social and Emotional Aspects of Learning) programme to help the social and emotional development of all children. (dcsf 2007)

4. At KS1, an able child from KS2 with similar interests might be co-opted as a friend or mentor. Similarly in secondary schools, older students are often very willing to perform a similar role. The befrienders and mentors will, of course, need some guidance and training.

5. The isolated themselves can be encouraged to act as mentors or befrienders to younger children or to help children in the class who are having difficulties with particular topics. Again, it will be necessary to offer some social training to isolated EA students before they attempt to do this kind of work so that they are aware of attitudes and behaviours that might act as barriers.

6. By bringing in someone from outside the school as a mentor. Many towns have branches of University of the Third Age (U3A). This is a wonderful source of highly educated people with a little time on their hands. One school used an ex-lecturer in history to work with an 8-year-old with a passion for archaeology. Meetings took place in the lunch hours and occasionally two other boys with similar interests joined them. The biggest problem for teachers was bringing these sessions to a close!

7. In secondary schools, it is often a sympathetic subject specialist who is most able to offer support to an EA student with similar interests.

8. Working with parents and carers is essential, especially where they are out of their depth with a child, or where it is possible that parental attitude is exacerbating difficulties or where excessive pressure to succeed is being applied.

9. Occasionally it may be necessary to offer more formal counselling to an isolated EA student. If the school is not able to offer this service, older students or parents could be directed to the National Association for Gifted Children (NAGC) helpline (0845 450 0295) or to the Youth section of its website. They might also be put in touch with Children of High Intelligence (CHI), an organization that offers advocacy services for the exceptionally able and their parents. Some EA pupils, who put themselves under huge pressure to achieve at the highest levels, will need help to accept that it is not necessary to produce perfect work every time (not everything will be worth the time and effort) and that occasional time-wasting is acceptable.

Teachers and the Exceptionally Able

The exceptionally able are hugely rewarding students for passionate subject-specialists and confident non-specialists to teach, but for the biologist, for example, who finds him/herself teaching advanced physics or the primary generalist, who has to deal with a computing or science prodigy, such students can appear time-consuming and threatening.

Teachers can best handle the exceptionally able by:

- admitting when they are out of their depth
- being prepared to learn from students
- being prepared to work with EA students to find the answers
- being flexible. In Freeman (2001:137) a student describes a supportive teacher who was prepared to work alongside the student and change her approach: 'I was the physics teacher's first A-level pupil, so she was always testing the water, saying, "Tell me, if I teach you this way, would you understand it better?" She was very flexible and tapped into me. It was good fun. When I wanted to take astronomy, at first the school said no, but I asked again and again, and eventually the teacher and I learnt it between ourselves, and that's how I came to study it at university'
- using the exceptionally able students' abilities for the benefit of other students
- boosting them up rather than putting them down.

Personalized Learning and Assessment

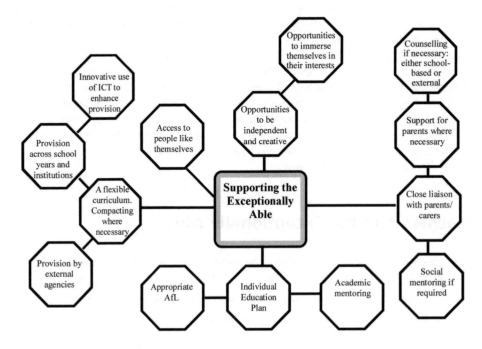

Supporting the Exceptionally Able

The learning needs of the exceptionally able are so different from those of most gifted and talented students that they are likely to need individually tailored programmes, especially if they are in schools with little experience of such students. Even where a school has a number of exceptional students, they are likely to have very different abilities or to be at different ages and stages. The aspiring ballet star or sprinter will have different needs from the computer whiz or advanced linguist.

Below are some of the key elements of provision for exceptionally able students.

Individual Education Plans

Where exceptionally able students need a highly individualized programme, it is essential that all its elements are pulled together in an IEP, which is drawn up and agreed by *all* the institutions involved, the parents and the students. Such an IEP will include targets for moving a student's learning forward as well as approaches to dealing with any areas of difficulty. The following is a suggestion of the kind of things that could be covered in an IEP together with a completed example.

Sample IEP for EA Students
Student Name and Year Group
Strengths • Rapidity of learning • Curiosity • Creativity • Problem-solving ability • Mathematical ability • Language ability • Sporting ability • Artistic ability (identify field) • Overwhelming interest in _____ • Leadership skills • Academic hunger
Areas for development • Ability to work with others • Spelling or handwriting • General presentation of work • Gross or fine motor skills • Participation in discussion • Motivation • Behaviour
Needs • Opportunities to work with pupils of similar ability whether academic or in a talent area • A markedly more advanced programme of work • Advanced specialist tuition • Opportunities to pursue an interest • Social interaction with those of similar intellectual ability • Barriers to learning to be overcome • Occasions to demonstrate strengths
Provision • Acceleration for particular parts of the curriculum • Mentoring, e-mentoring or counselling • Expertise from other areas of school or beyond • Individual homework programme • Enrichment of the curriculum • Opportunities beyond the school • A balanced programme of support and extension for those with dual exceptionality
Targets (termly or half-termly depending on the programme and resources available) • These should be quite specific

Individual Education Programme – An Example
Peter Smith, Year 4
The following programme has been agreed by Peter, his parents and the school with advice from the conservatoire and local secondary school.
Strengths   • Mathematical ability assessed at beyond Level 7 of the National Curriculum   • Self-taught pianist – identified by visiting orchestral group   • Highly motivated and eager to make progress
Areas for Development   • Shy – finds it difficult to socialize   • Diagrams and mathematical drawings need to be more accurate
Needs   • Security of remaining within existing class where he has a close friend   • Individualized mathematics programme   • External provision of specialist music tuition   • Encouragement to interact with others as well as his close friend
Provision   1. Year 9 maths programme put together by head of maths in local secondary school and delivered by Year 12 student from that school. He will visit primary school once a week and provide additional email support, monitored by head of mathematics.   2. Saturday scholarship awarded at local music conservatoire – piano and general musicianship.   3. Encouragement to use NRICH and other mathematical websites for further challenge.
Targets   1. To make more careful use of ruler and other equipment resulting in improved accuracy of geometric drawings and models.   2. To take GCSE maths at end of Year 4 and achieve an A Grade – (advised by secondary school that this is easily within his grasp; Peter has seen past papers and is confident of success).   3. At least weekly exchange of emails with Year 12 tutor (to encourage social interaction as well as supporting maths programme).   4. Weekly Saturday attendance throughout term at music conservatoire.   5. One school piano performance at end of first term (on advice of conservatoire)   6. First graded piano examination at end of second term (level to be decided by conservatoire).   Targets to be reviewed by leading teacher of gifted and talented, parents and Peter at the beginning of each term.

Note:

Such an IEP will need to be developed as part of a long-term plan for Peter. Continuity of provision is essential.

Extending and Enriching the Curriculum

The mother of Dominic (see case study on page 42), who had been accelerated one year and moved on to a top university early, expressed frustration on behalf of her son because he was never given the satisfaction of a challenging curriculum. It was too easy for him to get As. Neither GCSEs nor A Levels provided any excitement or buzz. There was no pleasure in going to school. This complaint amply demonstrates that acceleration alone may not be enough. EA students like this boy need programmes that:

- move way beyond the usual curriculum and explore topics and aspects of topics that are not usually covered
- may introduce additional subjects such as another language, astronomy or philosophy
- give them opportunities for carefully constructed and monitored independent study where they are pushed to the limits of their understanding
- inject excitement and challenge through discussion and debate with intellectual equals – which might mean looking beyond the school as in the two examples below.

Case Study

Every Tuesday, a very special group of KS2 students gathers at Bunbury Aldersey C of E Primary School in Cheshire. They come from ten surrounding primary schools and represent the top 1–2 per cent of the national ability range. With the support of DWS, the Day a Week School organization, these schools decided to meet the challenge posed by these exceptional students by giving them the opportunity to work with others of similar ability once a week on high level science and mathematics problems – the subjects that create most difficulties for non-specialist teachers in primary schools.

The identification process, which involved all KS2 children in the ten schools, was carefully devised so that prior teaching would not influence it. A multi-layered problem was given so that most children could access it on the first level but only the most able would be able to respond at the highest level. After moderating the results, likely candidates took part in workshops demanding practical, numerical, logical and philosophical problem solving. At this stage, the final list of DWS pupils was decided.

As well as working on science and mathematics problems, DWS students also do Philosophy for Children (P4C), team challenges, lateral thinking exercises and some independent work.

As long as students progress well they will stay in the group throughout Key Stage 2. All children who join any of the primary schools late, as well as students who teachers believe have been overlooked, are assessed each year and can join the group if this is considered appropriate.

When students move on to KS3, a report is sent to the receiving secondary schools. The nearest one is beginning to show interest in continuing the project.

Solving magic squares is one thing – but creating them and finding rules for creating them is quite another!

Case Study

Francesca was 14 when she wrote this.

The first thing I can remember about being remotely different from anyone else was in reception, when a Educational Psychologist came to speak to me, due to suspicions from teachers that I have been gifted. I sat in a corner, when this man came over and sat down with me. "Now Francesca, I want you to read this book for me." He had a strong Liverpool accent, so pronounced 'book' as if it rhymed with 'duke'. I looked at him, and simply said, "You mean book?" (Pronouncing it as it should be.) I shall never forget the look on his face, a look of astonishment, and also amusement, that a 4-year-old should correct an adult on their pronunciation.

It was not long after that, that I started going to extra literacy sessions with a teacher who came to work with special needs children. I would go out of the classroom with her and work on reading and writing skills, often reading books that the years high above me were starting on. These sessions continued all the way through my primary education, and looking back on them, I have many fond memories.

In the same year, I was encouraged to take up a musical instrument, and began learning to play the keyboard. In Y1, I used to go through to Y2 for literacy, in order to do the work that I was capable of. I didn't understand why I did it. By this time I had grown accustomed to doing things my peers didn't. After a while, I began going to Y6 for lessons, much to the amusement of the older children. When I reached Y2, my teacher carried out an experiment,

$\rightarrow$ *continued* . . .

and asked that I do my KS2 literacy SATs exam, as well as KS1, in reading and writing. I did, and got a level 5, the same level I would get in the real exam 4 years later.

In Y3 I started extra literacy lessons after school and KS3 Spanish at a local high school after school. At this stage, I also occasionally went to Y6 for literacy lessons. All these extra-curricular activities carried through until I was in Y6 myself, when I left school. I can quite honestly say that it was one of the most hectic school experiences anyone can have, but I enjoyed it immensely, till the very end.

Note:

Written as this is from the child's perspective, it is easy to overlook the detailed planning and consultation that the school carried out in order to cater for Francesca's needs. The primary school had a very inclusive approach, providing equally successfully for its SEN students as for the gifted.

Appropriate Assessment for Learning

As with all students, AfL is an important tool for improving the motivation of EA students and helping them to understand how to progress to the next level. However, it is important to recognize that some AfL strategies will not be appropriate for these students. For example, peer-assessment, where a student's level of achievement is years in advance of his/her peers, would be dispiriting for assessment partners and unhelpful for the EA student. A conversation with a teacher, teaching assistant, an older EA student or an exchange with an e-tutor will be much more useful in these circumstances (see Appendix 3). However, strategies such as 'three stars and a wish' where a peer identifies and comments on three good aspects of some work before making a 'wish' for how it could be improved, are just as useful when being applied by an adult to an EA student. Some EA students are excessively self-critical and need as much positive feedback as other students. An EA student in Freeman (2001:140) commented that teachers 'Never say, "Well done"'.

EA students should be able to play a major role in the assessment of their progress through self-assessment. They will, of course, need the tools such as clear agreed targets and National Curriculum level criteria (in child friendly language for younger students), but many will be able to tell the teacher when they think they have achieved a goal and are ready to move forward again.

Use of expertise from beyond the school

In many cases EA students will need access to expertise beyond the school. Sometimes, especially with younger students, it will be sufficient to approach a school or college in the next phase but there will be occasions when it is necessary to cast the net wider.

The dscf has a list of approved drama, dance and music schools for students of exceptional talent. Support for those with sporting talent is provided via the Sports Trust. Young, Gifted and Talented (YGT) provides access to a wide range of enrichment activities through its Learner Academy and its regional Excellence Hubs and advanced programmes are available for older pupils through the Open University. Professional organizations such as the Royal Society of Chemists, as well as charitable trusts such as the Arvon Foundation, which runs residential writing courses supported by professional writers, can provide challenge for EA students as well as opportunities to meet with others like themselves. Many EA students enjoy competition and there is a vast array of competitions in sciences, DT, ICT, mathematics and other subjects that can stimulate and motivate. (See Appendix 3 for a list of organizations that might offer support to EA students.)

A Flexible Curriculum

Where EA students are taking part in time-consuming and demanding activities outside school, it is important for all teachers to be aware of this and to take this into account when giving homework or setting deadlines for work. The Junior Athlete Education programme run by the Sports Youth Trust works with teachers and parents to make them aware of the pressures being placed on specific students with great sporting talent. (See case study on page 40 for an example of how one school supports such students.)

It would be wonderful if the same support could be offered to accommodate other EA students because, too often, they find themselves under pressure from all sides. A strong home/school partnership that allows parents to represent the interests of their children without undermining teachers is invaluable.

Some secondary school departments have supported EA students by allowing them to sit in on parts of departmental meetings and to contribute ideas on the most successful teaching approaches for them, how the curriculum could be modified to provide challenge and the resources they need. Such approaches must be as helpful to teachers as they are to the students involved.

Literacy

The Importance of Early Exposure to Books

When identifying factors that contribute to the underachievement of able children, low expectation is rightly at the top of the list. It, however, is closely followed by poor literacy skills and increasingly by limited access to or knowledge of ICT. Lack of early exposure to books and to conversation are major obstacles to developing good literacy skills as research carried out by Gordon Wells in Bristol showed.

> What is so important about listening to stories, then, is that, through this experience, the child is beginning to discover the symbolic potential of language: its power to create possible and imaginary worlds through words – by representing experience in symbols that are independent of the objects, events, and relationships symbolized and that can be interpreted in contexts other than those in which the experience originally occurred, if indeed it ever occurred at all.

He goes on to say that:

> Children who had been read to were better able to narrate an event, describe a scene, and follow instructions. But perhaps what was most important in accounting for teachers' higher assessment of these children's oral language abilities was the greater ease with which they appeared to be able to understand the teacher's use of language. (Wells 1987:156; 157)

Sharon, below, was a child for whom low familial expectation was further exacerbated by her limited experience of language on entering school.

Case Study

When Sharon was 5 she already had three younger siblings. Her mother had been pregnant when she left school without any qualifications. She lived on benefits and had difficulty managing her family. There was no support from any of the children's fathers. There were no books in the house and Sharon did not attend nursery because her gran looked after her whenever her mother went out. She was not taught to read or write her name before she went to school. Language at home was largely a matter of imperatives – 'Stop it!', 'Get yer coat on', 'Give the baby his bottle'. She watched a lot of adult afternoon television but was rarely allowed to watch any of the children's programmes because her mother found them boring.

→ *continued* . . .

> Her reception teacher noticed that Sharon appeared to be 'hungry' for stories and would listen intently, answering questions enthusiastically. She appeared to be very bright but did not know any nursery rhymes. Her lack of pre-school experience of books and language and her mother's unwillingness to listen to her reading after school meant that the gap between Sharon and other able children in the class started to grow.

By the time Sharon moves into secondary school, if she is to keep up with her able peers, she will need good literacy skills. Ideally she should be able to:

- demonstrate a high level of technical correctness in speech and writing
- write complex sentences using extensive vocabulary
- write and speak in a variety of registers and styles to suit audience
- identify and demonstrate irony, humour, absurdity, implied meanings
- experiment with plot and characters, displaying originality
- demonstrate speed and depth of understanding in the spoken and written word
- express and debate ideas in discussion
- select, extract and synthesize facts from a passage of writing
- read widely. (Based on Evans et al. 1997:20)

Obviously a comprehensive support package is required, not just in reception but throughout her schooling, if Sharon is to develop these skills and not become another able dropout. KS1 teachers are very good at remembering and taking into account children's early learning experiences in relation to literacy, the same is not always true of the teachers they meet at later stages.

Looking at the draft 'Classroom Quality Standards in Gifted and Talented Education' (DfES 2007:103), the key section for Sharon is 'Understanding Learners' Needs'. Below is an example of how the Exemplary standards might be used to meet Sharon's needs, initially in KS1.

Classroom Quality Standards in Gifted and Talented Education		
Understanding Learners' Needs	**Exemplary**	**What might this look like for Sharon?**
How well are the emotional and social needs of the learner identified and addressed?	Identification and review of gifted and talented learners use multiple criteria, performance and value-added data. Provision and its impact are regularly reviewed by professionals working collaboratively.	Sharon's progress is measured against her achievement on entering school – not in comparison with her peers. Her positive learner behaviours and curiosity are valued. A Raven's Coloured Progressive Matrices test reveals high underlying ability even though literacy skills are comparatively weak. The leading teacher of gifted and talented and SEN coordinator are involved in her support.

How well are barriers to learning identified and removed?	Comprehensive strategies counteract adverse social, organizational and curriculum pressure. Specialized focused support is provided for gifted and talented underachievers and those with exceptional ability or talent.	Sharon receives half an hour's individual tuition every day from the classroom assistant. She is often placed with the most able children so that she is exposed to their language and ideas. An education welfare officer visits the home and encourages the mother to become involved in the school. Sharon is given additional access to a computer for a phonics programme and so that she can hear and watch nursery stories and rhymes. She is encouraged to retell stories to her teacher and to learn some to tell her younger siblings. Books are readily supplied for her to take home.
How well is gifted and talented learners' progress assessed, monitored and evaluated in order to raise achievement?	Classroom practice regularly requires gifted and talented learners to reflect on progress against their targets and to determine the direction of their own learning. Assessment uses predictive data (local and national) from other subject areas.	Sharon has a special chart on which she records all the books she reads, a basic sight vocabulary and her Jolly Phonics progress. When she meets her targets she is rewarded with a sticker.
How well are the training and learning needs of teachers and classroom assistants identified in order that they can meet the needs of the learners?	Professionals share their knowledge (including from action research) and their analysis of what good gifted and talented provision looks like. This contributes to enhanced provision for gifted and talented learners in a 'community of learning' of teachers, parents/carers and pupils.	Leading teacher for gifted and talented talks informally in a staff meeting about barriers to learning and underachievement amongst gifted and talented students. Teachers discuss children who fall into this category and share ideas for helping them. There are plans for some action research in this area.

EAL Students and 'Head Words'

For gifted and talented students for whom English is an Additional Language (EAL) the literacy problems can be very different. Very often they will have parents who value education and expect them to work hard and make good progress. Usually they pick up the language quickly, especially in the playground, but then teachers are puzzled by their poor performance in assessments and tests as in the example below.

Case Study

> Abdus arrived in the UK as a refugee with his mother when he was 11 years old. He went to an inner city school that was accustomed to dealing with immigrants and made rapid progress with his English. His mother was determined that he would do well at school because she saw education as an escape route from poverty and repression. By the time he was in Year 10, Abdus was achieving well in the classroom but his examination performance was always much weaker. He tended to seize on key words and write everything he knew about those words regardless of the questions.

Abdus is the kind of boy that Ian Warwick and the REAL (Realizing Equality and Achievement for Learners) team at London Gifted and Talented are very familiar with. Their research led them to the conclusion that even though Abdus and others like him learn the key words of various subjects (e.g. in science, osmosis, forces, magnesium, Bunsen burner etc.) they do not understand what REAL calls 'head words'. These are the words necessary to interpret questions and tasks such as analyse, compare, apply, select or evaluate. Simply giving EAL students a list of examination questions and asking them to highlight the words they are unsure of reveals this problem. EAL students who speak English fluently may need additional subject and EAL specialist support to overcome this difficulty. (London Gifted and Talented 2008)

Literacy and Gifted and Talented Boys

Concern about the poor performance of boys in English relative to that of girls has been expressed for several years. The following table illustrates the huge gap in achievement over the last ten years.

Percentage of Boys and Girls Achieving grades A*–C in GCSE English			
Year	% Boys	% Girls	% Difference
1997	43	65	22
2002	48	64	16
2007	55.3	69.2	13.9

The good news is that the gap is slowly shrinking, possibly because teachers are beginning to understand the reasons for this poor performance but there is still a long way to go. Small-scale research was carried out at Calday Grange Grammar School on the Wirral with a group of eight Year 10 boys, who had achieved Level 8 in mathematics or science at KS3 and only Level 6 in English, and eight Year 8 boys who were predicted to achieve the same results. The boys were interviewed separately and the following explanations for the gap in performance between English and their maths and science were gathered:

1. They liked the way teachers modelled work on the blackboard and demonstrated techniques in science.
2. They enjoyed the practical hands-on experiences in science
3. The emotions involved in English made some of these boys uncomfortable. They prefer to approach life from a more objective perspective.
4. English failed to reflect their interests, especially their love of sport.
5. They preferred fact to fiction.
6. They did not always see English as relevant to their career choices.
7. They feared failure.
8. Some had difficulties with punctuation and spelling and disliked 'the lack of control in English, especially with writing mechanics'. (Darley and McGoldrick 2005)

This reinforces observations from other sources that it is not lack of ability that hampers boys' progress in literacy and English but a reluctance to engage with a subject that does not bring them much reward, does not fit in with their interests and does not provide sufficient opportunities to 'do'. The following figure shows some of the strategies that are likely to improve their performance.

Provide clearly set tasks with well-defined outcomes   More hands-on activities

More non-fiction books relevant to their interests

Defined outcomes   Shorter written tasks

For younger boys, let them read aloud to peers rather than to a teacher

Signal that boys' reading preferences are valued

More opportunities for discussion and debate

Use visual stimuli (DVDs, photographs, film clips), ICT and drama to aid writing tasks

Improving the Literacy Skills of Gifted and Talented Boys

Literacy for All Gifted and Talented Students

For all gifted and talented children to develop the literacy skills they need, they should be exposed to the following:

Reading

1. Longer more complex texts (including non-fiction)
2. Consideration of *how* as well as *what* they read
3. Inferential questioning
4. Discussion and high quality book talk
5. Awareness of an author's use of language
6. Time to reflect on their learning.

Writing

1. Clear objectives
2. Extended or modified objectives when necessary
3. Modelling the writing process, especially of more complex writing, through teacher demonstration or teacher scribing, explaining any decisions made
4. Use of individual whiteboards and markers to allow rapid drafting and redrafting of ideas and sharing of ideas with peers
5. Ability pairings for discussion, planning and peer-assessment
6. Knowledge and use of technical language – providing gifted and talented writers with the tools of the trade
7. References to the effect of writing on the reader
8. Probing questions about their writing
9. Development of the skills of literary criticism
10. Challenging group targets where they will have to cooperate
11. Use of a reading/writing journal for jotting down ideas and thoughts
12. Occasional opportunities to prepare and present a text for a lesson
13. Extended tasks over a number of sessions so that the most able can get 'stuck in' to a piece of written work.

Speaking and Listening

1. Different styles of speech for different occasions
2. Opportunities to articulate explanations, not just to present facts
3. Open-ended questions that encourage able students to give detailed responses
4. Modelling speech patterns
5. External speakers, visits to theatres, etc.

Good standards of literacy for gifted and talented students are important across the curriculum and all subject teachers and class teachers should take a part in providing them with the technical language required and in helping them to communicate effectively in speech and in writing. Reading Days or Poetry Days when teachers, governors, parents and others are encouraged to bring in and read from their favourite books are ideal opportunities for raising the status of reading among boys and making them aware that it is something that adult males do. Similarly, getting teachers and other adults to share the different kinds of writing that they do with boys may help to establish writing as a valuable skill.

ICT and the Digital Divide

The Digital Divide

Marc Prensky writes: 'It is amazing to me how in all the hoopla and debate these days about the decline of education in the USA we ignore the most fundamental of its causes. Our students have changed radically. Today's students are no longer the people our educational system was designed to teach.' (Prensky 2001)

He goes on to say that a 'discontinuity' has taken place since the rapid assimilation of digital technology in the latter half of the twentieth century. One outcome is that today's students think and absorb information in a different way from earlier generations. They can be regarded as 'digital natives' while very often their teachers and parents are 'digital immigrants' – people who have come in from the outside and have to learn a new language – the digital language. This discontinuity has occurred in the UK too and 'Digital Immigrant instructors, who speak an outdated language (that of the pre-digital), are struggling to teach a population that speaks an entirely new language'. (Prensky 2001)

What impact does this have on our most able students?

1. Students, even the very young ones, brought up using mobile phones, DVDs, video games, computers and other digital technology are accustomed to instant results; to processing several pieces of information at the same time; fun, excitement and adrenalin highs when they are learning new computer games; and accessing information whenever they want it. In comparison, standard classroom teaching is slow and boring. Some able students turn off in the classroom or even opt out of school early in search of experiences more relevant to their lives.
2. Today's able students become impatient and lose respect for their 'digital immigrant' teachers as they struggle to keep up. They cannot understand why so much is printed off rather than being read from the computer. They cannot understand why their teachers do not take the shortcuts offered by technology. They cannot understand why they are not allowed to use the resources they have at hand, such as mobile phones. They cannot really see the point of school when it is so old-fashioned.

3. Students from homes that do not have access to digital technology are themselves 'digital immigrants' and as such are at a huge disadvantage in comparison with their more affluent peers. This is another factor contributing to the underachievement of poorer able students. Research carried out by the LSE among 1,500 9–19 year olds found that 'children from better-off backgrounds not only had greater access to the world wide web at home but were more likely to exploit its array of resources'. (Ward 2005)

How do digital immigrant teachers cope with very able students whose ICT skills are far in advance of their own and what can they do to help them, given that they have less knowledge than the student?

1. Accept that the teacher/student relationship has been turned on its head and be prepared to learn from the students. If this is done with a good grace, a 'learning together' atmosphere can be fostered in the classroom.
2. In some cases, digital technology skills far outstrip a student's ability to explain what s/he can do. Getting these students to plan and give a lesson on a particular process, can be useful to the class and encourage the able student to sort and present ideas in an effective manner.
3. When planning group activities that require the use of digital technology, make sure that there is a digitally accomplished student in each group so that they make best use of their resources.
4. If these students are eager to help, allow them to help set up technological resources for lessons.
5. Sometimes, these students' computing skills are very much more advanced than their conventional writing skills. Teachers will need tact and humour to ensure that steps are taken to redress this imbalance

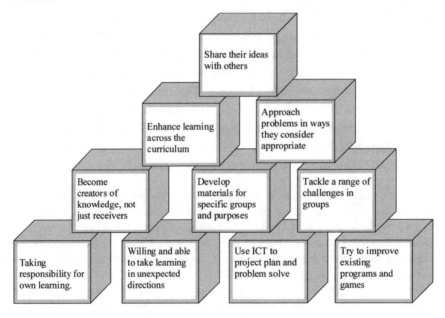

Using ICT to Develop Independent Learning Skills

Harnessing Troublesome Technology

Making good use of digital technology is central to personalizing the curriculum so that the most able can work at a pace and on materials appropriate to them. It should not be regarded as an 'add-on' but should be fully integrated into all aspects of school life. Teachers also need to embrace some of the technology that is currently seen as a threat to discipline and achievement rather than as a valuable resource. The following case study is an example of an ICT teacher who did this to good effect.

Mobile Phones

Case Study

Daniel Ellison from Little Heath School in Reading persuaded a mobile phone company to lend the school mobile phones with video facilities.

He used these resources in a number of ways:

1. Getting students to take short clips on a given theme, putting the clips together and editing them with the support of local video journalists, who also explained the ethics of this kind of journalism.
2. Asking students to take videos, still photos or sound clips of examples of whatever they are studying.
3. Putting together clips from idea '2' into a file and using them as a range of examples to demonstrate certain concepts, or as categorization exercises.
4. Asking students to make a short (30-second video) on a relevant topic before transferring it to another student by email, media messenger or computer. This student then creates another clip to follow.
5. Asking students to create a programme designed especially for mobile phones, such as an advert or revision tip. Students might research what they are doing, write a script and draw a storyboard before videoing it.
6. Setting a homework task that involves the students videoing a short clip and sending it back to the school.
7. Making video postcards.
8. Establishing video pals in other parts of the country or world using texting.

(Ellison 2007)

There have been problems with the misuse of mobiles in schools but it might be better to get students making educational use of them rather than recording 'happy slapping' and other unsavoury incidents.

Computer Games

Another digital resource regarded with suspicion is the computer game. This is understandable given the violence of some of the games on sale, but tapping into this resource by presenting challenging information in game form can enable students to grasp difficult concepts that they might not be able to grasp through more conventional approaches. Again Marc Prensky provides an example of this. A group of professors came to his company with CAD software they had developed. College students were finding it difficult to master so they wanted to explore making it into a game. The professors wanted to teach the various skills in linear fashion and had made movies of five to ten minutes to illustrate various points. They were persuaded to inject faster pace, shorten the movies to 30 seconds, allow random rather than step-by-step access to the various tasks and jettison written instructions. The game was a huge success and students engaged with concepts that they had previously found too difficult.

British schools and City Learning Centres like the one in Camden, London are beginning to tune into the potential of 3D game authoring tools, teaching able students first how to use them and then using the feedback to assess how game technology could be used to both motivate and get across difficult concepts in other subject areas. These are exciting developments for our able students.

ICT for the Most Able Students

Our most able students should be encouraged to develop as independent learners by using ICT, including emerging technologies to:

- become creators of knowledge not just receivers (games, presentations, websites, blogs)
- take responsibility for their own learning and tackle tasks in ways that seem appropriate to them
- take their learning in unexpected directions with the guidance of teacher questioning
- project plan and problem solve
- pmprove existing games and programmes
- develop materials for specific groups or purposes
- tackle a range of challenges in groups
- enhance their learning across the curriculum
- share ideas with others.

The QCA website includes some examples of how units of work at KS1 and KS2 can be extended to cater for the most able pupils in the class through the use of open-ended higher order questioning and more detailed analysis and development of tasks. One is based around Unit 6a 'Multimedia Presentation' where the majority of the class will be working towards producing a simple multimedia presentation. Ideas for how this could be developed can be found below and are expanded further at QCA (2007).

> ## *Extending Unit 6a 'Mulitmedia Presentation'*
>
> Able pupils could be asked:
>
> 1. How are different forms of information combined for particular audiences in television, websites, computer games and CD-Roms (images, typeface, layout, use of animation, voice-over and soundtracks)?
> 2. What images and styles are used for different age groups and genders?
> 3. What types of music are used and what effects does the music create?
> 4. What is the tone of voice of the commentary?
> 5. How is the author trying to influence or persuade?
> 6. Do images and sound always complement each other?
>
> Pupils should then be asked to apply this understanding to their own presentations which could be on a controversial topic, such as animal testing or global warming. They could produce two presentations – one supporting the issue and one against it – after collecting a range of media, possibly including video, to illustrate their ideas.

The impact of digital technology on the opportunities for able students with disabilities and those from different cultures is incalculable. The use of word processors for dyslexics, tablets and synthesized voices for the blind and masses of visual resources for the deaf has uncovered a range of gifts and talents whose development had been inhibited by disability. Teachers with disabled students in their classes will need to seek advice on the best ICT resources to use with them. Able EAL students as well as those from different cultures find ICT a powerful communication tool.

ICT is an essential tool for the personalization of the curriculum. Where an exceptionally able student might have been considered for acceleration to an older age group, creative use of ICT to develop challenging activities can make this unnecessary and allow the student to stay with his/her peers if this is the preferred outcome.

ICT – Ethics and Dangers

At the same time as able students are being encouraged to use ICT imaginatively, they will have to be taught about computer law, ethics and dangers. Very often able students' ability to use technology outstrips their awareness of what is legal and what is acceptable. They will need to know about:

1. Data Protection. Older students could research this and make an original and lively presentation for pupils and staff.
2. Computer viruses and worms.
3. Plagiarism. Younger children could be given a piece of work and asked to identify where passages had been cut and pasted together from different sources.
4. The dangers of giving out too much personal data over the internet. A playlet written and acted by pupils is more likely to have an impact than a lecture from a teacher.
5. Computer ethics – using video journalists to do this would be effective.
6. Cyber-bullying – this can appear to be harmless fun to the perpetrators unless it is specifically included in a school's anti-bullying policy.
7. Hacking – the potential penalties.

ICT – Links with Home

Digital technology is being used in some schools to keep parents up to date with their children's progress so they can go online and look at their latest marks and their attendance record. This means that if an able student begins to slip back and underachieve, parents are alerted to it straight away and can try to identify a cause rather than wait until the termly or yearly parents' evening. Parents can also find out what homework has been set so the disorganized able child can be chivvied into doing it. Increasingly homework can be submitted online, a big incentive to boys who dislike doing anything on paper. While these approaches are laudable, it does, of course, mean that able students whose parents are not online are again disadvantaged.

More and more schools are investing in sturdy laptops that students can take home or use around the school and there are even examples of parents being offered financial help to go online. Measures like this are essential if the digital divide is not to increase the disadvantage already experienced by students from poor homes.

6 Gifted and Talented Students with Additional Needs

There are many potentially able students who, for a wide variety of reasons, may underachieve. Some of these students are referred to as having double exceptionality and more recently the term dual or multiple exceptionality (DME) has been coined to cover those who have several conditions. For example, a student who is potentially very able may also have both visual impairment and behavioural problems. Others do not have a recognized condition but are limited by their environment or personal circumstances. In this chapter all these students will be referred to as having additional needs.

These additional needs fall into five main groups:

- physical or sensory deprivation
- specific learning difficulties
- behavioural or mental problems
- social and economic disadvantage
- Black and Minority Ethnicity (BME) and English as an additional language (EAL).

Although each group has different disadvantages and needs, concentrating first and foremost on finding out what these students are good at – or could be good at – will alleviate much of the stress and frustration of those who feel that teachers and other adults focus only on their limitations. Examples of good practice can be found. The National Talent Framework for PE and Sport has explicit plans for recognizing talented students within the disabled population. (Youth Sports Trust 2008) If other curriculum devisers can be persuaded to adopt a similar approach, then untapped talents, gifts and abilities may emerge.

Physical or Sensory Deprivation

For all students with physical or sensory deprivation there is a common problem, whether they are very able or not, and that is that our society tends to adopt a medical model, focusing on the disability to the detriment of any possible gifts and talents. The problem is exacerbated by identification strategies that concentrate on verbal and normal communication skills when some of these students do not find it easy to develop these skills.

Blind and Visually Impaired Students

The abilities of blind and partially sighted students are often underestimated and they underperform because:

1. Teachers rarely have experience of teaching gifted and talented with visual problems.
2. Most identification tools are inadequate. These students will be disadvantaged when schools use CATs and other standardized tests as the basis for selection for gifted and talented programmes.
3. There may be developmental delay, especially in spatial awareness.
4. There may be communication problems with their sighted peers, which can undermine confidence and performance.
5. Unintended prejudice may exclude these students from gifted and talented programmes.
6. Funding can be a problem because of the additional resources and support needed.

Where it is difficult to assess the potential of visually impaired students, the Nebraska Starry Night model described in Chapter 2, which focuses on personality and behaviours such as humour, curiosity and engagement, is likely to be much more useful than standard assessment methods. A Parent Nomination Form like the one below modified from Montgomery (2003:104) might also draw attention to behaviours that teachers have not noticed.

PARENT NOMINATION FORM	
Characteristics	✓ if it applies
Recalls facts easily	
Has a long attention span, is persistent and sticks to tasks	
Has advanced vocabulary, expresses self fluently and clearly	
Is an avid reader (if provided with appropriate format)	
Curious	
Has a wide range of interests	
Reasons well	
Asks reasons why – questions almost everything	

Seeks own answers and solutions to problems	
Is independent and self-sufficient	
Sets self high goals	
Follows complex directions	
Enjoys complicated games	
Likes 'grown up' things and to be with older people	
Has a great interest in the future and world problems	
Has a good sense of humour	
Tends to dominate others if given the chance	
Is a leader	
Shows initiative	
Thinks quickly	
Wants to know how things work	
Is adventurous	
Puts unrelated ideas together in new and different ways	

Once abilities have been identified, teachers should make sure they have a clear idea of the nature of the impairment (e.g. tunnel vision, extreme short-sightedness, no sight whatsoever) before devising strategies to present the curriculum in appropriate ways. This might involve:

1. Looking at written material and whiteboards from the viewpoint of a visually impaired student and asking whether text size, font, colour and colour of background are appropriate for that particular student.
2. Providing access to Braille and Braille writers where this is more suitable than computer technology or where students are more comfortable with this resource.
3. Encouraging them to work with sighted students.
4. Getting them to use recording devices to devise games, quizzes and questionnaires that can be used by sighted classmates so that they are encouraged to socialise.
5. Making good use of modern digital technology. For example, the Talking Tactile Tablet devised in association with RNCB is suitable for all age groups. Students get instant audio feedback when they touch, for example, a tactile map, diagram or chart. There is a menu through which they can access additional data as and when they need it. By using resources such as these, forcing able blind students into a restricted curriculum can be avoided.
6. Ensuring that they have the same access to gifted and talented programmes as other students even if this does demand additional supervision and modification of materials.
7. Working through their strengths as much as possible and making peers aware of these so that the blind student does not feel inferior to sighted peers.
8. Trying to bring high-achieving blind role models into school.

Deaf Students

The degree to which deafness impairs gifted performance will depend on whether it is congenital, total, partial or whether it developed in childhood as, for example, a complication to another illness like meningitis. In recent years the signing/speaking debate has continued to rumble on with some specialist schools and teachers insisting on deaf students trying to speak while others allow signing and still others go for a mixed economy approach. Many deaf students prefer to sign, using British Sign Language or Makaton, but this means that they cannot communicate with hearing peers unless they too learn to sign. This isolation can produce a sort of identity crisis that many resolve by identifying with an entirely separate Deaf culture, in which they have confidence and can achieve. They may indeed reject tags such as gifted and talented because they interfere with their views of themselves as separate.

High ability in deaf students is often overlooked because:

1. Deafness is not always identified in toddlers. If they do not appear very responsive, parents and health workers may attribute this to lack of ability.
2. Some have been forced into speaking when they would have found signing easier. Being denied the opportunity to communicate in their preferred medium often masks ability.
3. Hearing peers do not always provide encouragement and support for deaf students and may inhibit their attempts at self-expression.
4. Frustration can provoke challenging behaviour that teachers tend to focus on, without considering the cause.

Any school that receives a deaf or partially hearing student should take steps to assess their potential, using strategies that do not focus on language. Suitable tools might be Raven's Coloured Progressive Matrices or Nebraska Starry Night profile, both described in Chapter 2. Where CATs and similar tests are used, teachers should look out for a spiky profile. For example, if verbal scores are low or average but numerical and/or non-verbal scores are higher, this could suggest an able student who is being hampered by his language problems. Further investigation and support would then be necessary. Identification of high ability in deaf students is essential if the problems identified by Vernon and La Falce-Landers (1993:433) are to be avoided: 'That nearly 40 percent (of able deaf students) required mental health treatment speaks to what happens when a brilliant intellect is confined by the double condition of deafness and inadequate opportunity.'

High ability in deaf students can be fostered by:

1. Providing them with tools to compensate for their disability e.g. word processors, VeeSee and similar TV channels which provide news, information and films in BSL, text-messaging, email, PowerPoint and interactive whiteboards.

2. Allowing them to teach BSL to small groups of hearing pupils (and teachers). This could be done during school or as an after-school club. Even young children will be able to do this and many hearing peers would enjoy the challenge.
3. Emphasizing their strengths and working through them as much as possible e.g. if they have a strong naturalist intelligence (as in Gardner's Multiple Intelligences) change the focus of some tasks so that they can use this knowledge and interest.
4. Highlighting their abilities rather than their disabilities to hearing peers.
5. Bringing high-achieving deaf role models into the classroom. Unfortunately, there are relatively few such role models for students to emulate.
6. Where there is setting across a year or grouping within a class, giving able deaf students access to higher groups and sets for some of their work, even if there are language difficulties.
7. Providing enrichment opportunities where their interests and abilities are strongest.
8. Offering additional support at any transition stage and during adolescence when behaviour difficulties may emerge.

Physical Disabilities

Whatever the nature of the disability, the principles in terms of identification of high ability and its nurturing are the same as those for sensory deprivation – look for what students can do rather than at the disability and then explore ways, using both human resources and technology, of allowing them to access the curriculum and work with peers to enhance both their learning and to encourage socialization. Jean-Dominique Bauby wrote a remarkable book, *The Diving Bell and the Butterfly*, after he suffered a severe stroke and was able to communicate by nodding and blinking one eye. Every day his scribe would arrive at the hospital and begin to jot down his story letter-by-letter:

> It is a simple enough system. You read off the alphabet (ESA version, not ABC) until with a blink of my eye I stop you at the letter to be noted. The manoeuvre is repeated for the letters that follow so that fairly soon you have a whole word, and then fragments of more or less intelligible sentences. That at least is the theory. (Bauby 2008:28)

There must be many potentially able students whose abilities are locked in bodies that do not work in the normal fashion. Finding ways of unlocking these abilities is essential for the mental well-being and fulfilment of the students and extremely satisfying for those involved in this process.

Specific Learning Difficulties

The term Specific Learning Difficulty is often used interchangeably with dyslexia but, in fact, it covers a range of verbal and non-verbal conditions, including dyslexia, dyspraxia and dysgraphia. As there is some evidence that dyslexia and dysgraphia can be linked with high ability, these are the conditions that will be dealt with here. Silverman (1989:37–42) found that a third of gifted and talented students in one sample had learning disabilities.

Dyslexia

Many highly able dyslexics are referred to educational psychologists for emotional and behavioural problems rather than learning difficulties. Why is this? Very often, it is because their high ability allows them to mask their problems and keep up with the class, but they become very frustrated, knowing that they are capable of much higher performance, wanting more challenging tasks and knowing that teachers (and sometimes parents) are underestimating them. This is when the behaviour problems are likely to develop. Attitudes to dyslexics in schools and society are changing. The different perspectives and creativity that dyslexics often bring to problem solving are becoming recognized as advantages in fields such as computing, design technology and science and their verbal communication skills can be an asset in the commercial world.

The table below highlights some of the characteristics of dyslexics that can contribute to underperformance and social difficulties. It also draws attention to some of the positive attributes that dyslexics may have. Obviously, no two dyslexics are the same. None is likely to show all the positive as well as all the negative qualities shown below. It is still a difficult condition to pin down.

Negative Characteristics of Dyslexia	Positive Attributes of Dyslexics
Poor reading, spelling and handwriting relative to their age and ability	Good memories
Some can read quite well but spelling is particularly poor in any situation where they are forced to write quickly	Good communication skills and wide vocabulary
Find sequencing activities challenging	Good spatial reasoning
Poor organizational skills	Often able to see the whole picture more easily than non-dyslexics
Find multiple instructions confusing	Intuitive learners
May be impulsive, aggressive or speak out when others would keep quiet	Good creative expressive ability

Can be oversensitive and have trouble socializing	Often have wide interests or deep knowledge of one subject
May refuse to work on anything that is found to be difficult	Often high ability in mathematics, science, design technology, computing, art or music
May have low frustration threshold	Often displays higher order thinking

Case Study

I was 14 when I was diagnosed dyslexic. My mum had told my primary school that she thought I was dyslexic as I hated reading and couldn't spell; she and my brother are also dyslexic so it was likely. My primary school, however, decided (and repeatedly told both myself and my parents) that there was nothing wrong with me, that I was just lazy and not very intelligent. One teacher even went as far as to make me spell both simple and difficult words (which I would inevitably get wrong) in front of the whole class so everyone could have a good laugh at my expense. She didn't do this with anyone else. That was pretty much every week as I didn't usually do too well on the weekly spelling tests. One occasion that is very vivid is there was a work sheet with no name on it, and instead of asking whose it was, this teacher waited until the whole class was quiet then asked me how to spell the number two. I said t-o-w. Everyone laughed (including her) she gave me the sheet and told me to sit down. This was when I was 7–9 years old and actually led to bullying by other students as they saw me as an 'easy target' and the teacher had shown there was nothing wrong with it.

It affects my learning quite a lot. I struggle reading black on white text. This often means that any notes we get given take me twice as long to read as everyone else and I can't easily read most textbooks to revise from. I end up making my own notes using a lot of colour. A lot of the teachers write in black on the board and I often have to ask my friend to read it out loud to me. I get words mixed up when we have to do dictation, and often can't read my own handwriting at all, because it is so poor.

Teachers that have helped have been the ones I have particularly got on well with, like my GCSE English teacher and physics teachers. When I started my GCSE years I was predicted a C in English, but I got an A* because this teacher gave me extra help when I needed it, and gave me confidence in my ability and myself. She also shut up the people who made fun of my spelling, which helped a lot as it started to undo the mindset my primary school had put me in that I was a 'retard'. My physics teachers also helped, and are the *only* teachers to have ever given me extra time on in-class tests, and made sure I could read things, and one of them even gave me a small piece of coloured glass to read through when the green plastic sheet that I used became unusable. I wasn't 'taught' to mind map properly until Year 11. I was never given an alternative way to present information, or note taking.

What help have I needed but not got? I needed to know I wasn't just thick, because up until I was diagnosed at 14 that's what I believed. I needed someone to tell me it was alright to not be able to read as well as everyone else. I needed them, once I had been diagnosed, to

→ *continued*...

not call my name out with a list of others to stay behind after assembly to organize extra time in exams, which involved a lot of embarrassment. I didn't want my whole year knowing. I needed to feel I wasn't being punished and shouldn't be ashamed of my dyslexia. On the learning levels someone with legible writing to take notes for me or a laptop, not having to do so much dictation quite so fast. Doing homework and school work could take me a lot longer than everyone else, so some proper support would have been beneficial; but also not being held back.

In my maths GCSE, which I took with the other fast trackers in November Year 11, I got 198/200 (though in coursework, which involved a lot of writing and I got no extra help with, I lost a third of the marks). I was using A-Level physics text books in Year 9. If they'd just let me work to the best of my ability, and not held me back so much, I would have had more confidence in myself. I know I'm smarter than most of my peers, but I got *no* encouragement and didn't find school academically challenging (except in English, which fast became my favourite subject alongside art for this reason). In some lessons, if I was too far ahead of the class, I would be told to do some homework for another subject. But not until I started to do well in my A-Level course did I ever get a 'well done' or told that what I was achieving was anything other than average; apart from the English teacher I mentioned. She kept encouraging me and giving me more advanced things to think about, such as suggesting reading material like Salman Rushdie, which resulted in my newly discovered passion for reading and writing; I'm currently in the middle of writing a trilogy.

Liz

Support Strategies for Able Dyslexic Students

1. First and foremost, provide for the gift or talent as well as for the disability.
2. Use humour as a way in – not laughing at but with. Many dyslexics have a keen ear for nuances in language and respond well to satire, puns and other word play.
3. Show the big, holistic picture first so that they understand why they are being asked to do something.
4. Spelling should be rule-based rather than lists of words to be rote learnt. They should be encouraged to analyse words and look for words they know within words, e.g. passion as pass-i-on.
5. A flowing cursive style of writing is more helpful than printing.
6. If a student is easily distracted, they should be allowed to use headphones (or walkman) to cut out sound or moved to the front of the class where they can be kept on task.
7. Teachers need to check that all homework and assignments are written down.
8. Ask students to repeat instructions – taking care not to humiliate them in front of their peers – and encourage them to talk through a problem aloud.
9. Use a wide range of teaching and learning strategies and allow a hands-on approach as much as possible.
10. In upper primary and secondary schools, use recordings, photocopies and close procedure to ease pressure associated with note taking.
11. In primary schools, a multi-sensory approach to reading and spelling might be helpful.
12. Teach study skills such as sequencing, highlighting key points, using different colours as a code, concept and mindmapping.

13. Provide plenty of scaffolding and structured work sheets.
14. Where necessary, teach social skills. It might be appropriate for a learning mentor to do this.
15. Encourage the development of word-processing skills and, even from an early age, allow them to submit some word-processed assignments so that they can concentrate on content.
16. Allow extra time when the mechanics of reading, writing and spelling slow students down.
17. Use rhythm, music and mnemonics to help students to remember vital information.
18. In group work, allow them to use their good memories by letting them report back from the group.

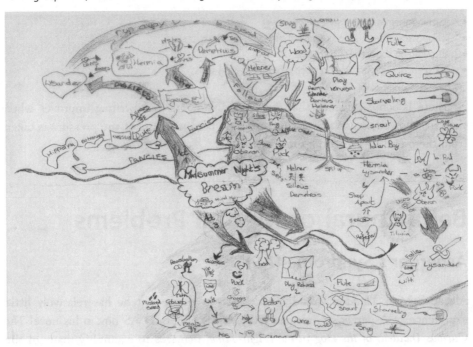

A mindmap created by a dyslexic 14-year-old to help him remember the key points and characters in *A Midsummer Night's Dream*

Notice the use of colour. He used blue shading for the labourers to designate loyalty and green shading (at the bottom) as that colour was associated with fairy characters. Each character has a different symbol.

Dysgraphia

Children who, having had good teaching and plenty of practice, are still unable to write neatly may be termed dysgraphic. This can be a very disabling condition because:

- teachers may not recognize underlying ability if the writing is difficult to decipher
- the effort involved in writing may get in the way of students' attempts to express themselves and stifle creativity

- if teachers set a high priority on neatness, dysgraphic students may get left behind because they have to work slowly to produce acceptable writing
- constant criticism for untidiness is not motivating and some students may begin to underachieve.

Some dysgraphic students are very able and in some cases there appears to be a link with dyslexia. They can be helped by:

- teaching them a cursive style of writing
- seeking advice from an occupational therapist in serious cases
- encouraging correct sitting posture
- being encouraged to develop good word-processing skills.

There is some evidence that dysgraphic students' handwriting improves when they are allowed to use a computer, possibly because some of the pressure is taken from them and they become more confident.

Behavioural or Mental Problems

Asperger's Syndrome (AS)

Although Mark Haddon would be the first to admit that he has relatively little experience of Asperger's syndrome (AS), Christopher, an AS boy in his novel *The Curious Incident of the Dog in the Night-Time*, manages to exemplify many of the characteristics of those suffering from this condition as shown in the two extracts below.

> The next day I saw 4 yellow cars in a row on the way to school which made it a black day so I didn't eat anything at lunch and I sat in the corner of the room all day and read my A level Maths course book. And the next day, I saw 4 yellow cars in a row on the way to school which made it another black day too, so I didn't speak to anyone and for the whole afternoon I sat in the corner of the library groaning with my head pressed into the join between the two walls and this made me feel calm and safe. But on the third day I kept my eyes closed all the way to school until we got off the bus because after I have had 2 black days in a row I'm allowed to do that.
>
> So I went up to the man in the little shop and I said, 'Where is 451c Chapter Road, London NW2 5NG?'
>
> And he picked up a little book and handed it to me and said, 'Two ninety-five.'
>
> And the book was called *LONDON AZ Street Atlas and Index Geographers A-Z Map Company* and I opened it up and it was lots of maps.
>
> And the man in the little shop said, 'Are you going to buy it or not?'

And I said, 'I don't know.'

And he said, 'Well, you can get your dirty fingers off it if you don't mind,' and he took it back from me.

And I said, 'Where is 451c Chapter Road, London NW2 5NG?'

And he said, 'You can either buy the A to Z or you can hop it. I'm not a walking encyclopaedia.'

And I said, 'Is that the A to Z?' and I pointed at the book.

And he said, 'No, it's a sodding crocodile.'

And I said, 'Is that the A to Z?' because it wasn't a crocodile and I thought I heard wrongly because of his accent. (Haddon 2004:68; 209)

Neihart (2000) identified seven characteristics that AS students share with *some* exceptionally gifted students. They appear in the left hand column below. The right hand column identifies the main differences between the two.

Characteristics shared by *some* exceptional gifted students and Asperger's syndrome sufferers	Additional characteristics of AS sufferers that mark them out from some of the exceptionally gifted
Verbal fluency and excellent memory	Pedantic seamless speech e.g. notice the flatness of Christopher's speech in the extract above
Fascination with letters/numbers – enjoys rote learning	Low tolerance to change e.g. even a different brand of baked beans could cause upset
Absorbing interest in specific topic	No understanding of humour e.g. Christopher did not understand the comment about the crocodile
Annoys peers with limitless talk about interests	Clumsiness in 50–90 per cent of cases
Asks awkward questions and gives lengthy discourses in response to questions	Inappropriate behaviour and lack of insight e.g. laughing when someone is distressed.
Hypersensitivity to sensory stimulation e.g. noise, colour, touch	Stereotypical behaviours and rituals (e.g. refusing to speak or eat if he sees yellow cars)
Extraordinary skills in a special area but possibly only average in others	

Support Strategies for Asperger's Syndrome (AS) Students

1. Teach directly the rules of social conduct, for example, in the dinner queue, you stand behind the person in front and don't ask for your dinner until s/he has been served.
2. Use stories, tapes, comic strips, pictures and demonstration to show the behaviour expected. Draw attention to desirable behaviours in peers.
3. Allow them time to pursue their special strengths and interests but limit questions and explanations that go on too long.
4. AS students may need support during breaks and lunch-hours. Some schools operate a buddy system using older students. Alternatively, provide access to a supervised area such as a library or computer room.

5. Be aware and make sure peers are aware of situations that make an AS student nervous e.g. being touched, moving him/her to another desk, sudden loud noises, unfamiliar people. A space where they can calm down is desirable.

6. Always prepare the student for any change of routine, such as a school trip, and make sure that supervision by a familiar person is provided.

7. Bear in mind that although an AS student may be exceptional at manipulating numbers, s/he is likely to find a problem-solving approach much more difficult. Try to be as concrete as possible when introducing new material and allow plenty of hands-on learning.

8. Similarly, AS students may learn to recognize words and read very early but find comprehension of what they are reading much more difficult. Tasks will need to be broken down into smaller steps.

9. In some cases, writing speed is slow so shorter class and homework assignments might be desirable.

10. Use visual clues as often as possible to demonstrate desired outcomes in both work and behaviour.

11. Build up self-esteem and confidence by giving them tasks that allow them to show off their good memories.

12. Try to make peers proud of an AS student's achievements, For example, they are often good at chess. Make sure that if they represent the school, they are praised for helping the school.

13. There may be difficulties in PE and games because of clumsiness and an inability to make sense of the rules. A fitness programme where they are trying to beat their own scores might be more motivating.

14. Inflexibility and strong reactions to sensory stimulation can make AS students very stressed. Sometimes, earplugs or a quiet place to work can help.

15. Additional support will be needed at each transition point.

Attention Deficit Hyperactivity Disorder (ADHD)

Whether or not this is a specific learning difficulty, a mental condition or a behavioural problem is still being debated. In some circles it is attributed to poor parenting but most evidence suggests that this is not the case. On the other hand, there does appear to be a genetic element in many instances. So what are the characteristics of this condition? Several of the following behaviours are likely to be present:

- attention span is very limited
- noticeably more restless and active than other children
- impulsive and seemingly unaware of danger
- needs instant gratification and attention
- moves from one activity to another without completing any
- non-stop chatter
- very sensitive to criticism
- finds it difficult to stick to rules
- behavioural problems exist in most settings, not just in lessons they do not like
- unpopular with peers because of unpredictable behaviour and tendency to 'muscle-in' on others' activities
- homework and equipment for lessons are often lost
- impatient with detail.

According to Montgomery (2003:83) gifted students with ADHD 'tend to show precocious motor development, intense interest in certain topics, problems following up school work and difficulties with peers'. Gifted ADHD students can be so difficult to manage, both at home and in the classroom, that it is easy to overlook their more positive attributes:

> An association is beginning to be made between creativity and ADD. For creativity to occur the conditions needed are a willingness to take risks, intrinsic motivation, tolerance of ambiguities, independence of thought and a belief in oneself despite what others say, the ability to redefine and look at problems from different perspectives – lateral thinking, skills of insight in which unusual connections between things can be made – and the strength of motivation to overcome barriers and obstacles (Hartman 2000). (Montgomery 2003:86)

If these students are to be catered for in schools, some elements of containment will be needed (such as seating them near the teacher, having a time-out zone and having very clear parameters for what is acceptable behaviour) but they will also need opportunities and encouragement to develop their creative talents through:

- problem-solving activities with a high level of challenge
- opportunities for self-direction
- high expectations and praise/reward for work and behaviour
- individual projects on topics that interest them
- concentration on higher level thinking skills
- some freedom in pace at which they work on a chosen activity
- high level discussion.

It may be necessary to draw peers into helping the ADHD student. In a Year 2 classroom, the author observed all the children join the teacher in giving a thumbs-up to an ADHD classmate who had sat through a story without wandering off. He was obviously delighted with this support.

Sometimes teachers pressure parents to put students, whom they suspect suffer from ADHD, on a drug programme such as Ritalin. In reality, there are several kinds of ADHD and Ritalin and similar drugs are not suitable for all kinds. In any case, hyperactivity in the classroom is not necessarily ADHD and a full assessment needs to be carried out before a diagnosis is made (see case study below).

Case Study

Andrew (Year 3) attended a fee-paying school. He was very musical and had already passed some grade exams for piano and violin. Sport was another passion. He played football every weekend and liked to swim. Maths lessons were a joy to him because the teacher recognized his high ability and kept him fed with a variety of challenging tasks. Everyone who met Andrew agreed that he was very bright, lively and challenging. Unfortunately he could not get on with the teacher who taught English, who also happened to be the deputy headteacher. He found her lessons very boring and whenever he tried to ask a question or raise a query about a book or story, she told him very firmly to be quiet. His handwriting was not good so she made him write out some pieces of work several times. Andrew became resentful and difficult in her lessons. When she started to send him out of the room, he entertained himself by pulling faces and making the class laugh.

Under pressure from the deputy head, the headteacher invited the mother in to the school and told her that she had a choice. She could go to her doctor and ask for Andrew to be prescribed Ritalin or she should take him away from the school. As there had never been complaints about Andrew's behaviour before, his mother opted to take him away and he joined the local state school. There were no further serious complaints about behaviour.

Social and Economic Disadvantage

Looked After Students

In 2006, of the 66,000 Year 8 students on the National Gifted and Talented Register, only 110 were looked after children. This is hardly surprising given that many of them move from school to school as one foster placement finishes and another begins. Their paper trails are often incomplete and teachers do not always have time to get to know them before they move on again. GCSE results for this group of children give more telling figures. Only 12 per cent of looked after children currently achieve five good GCSEs. In the general school population some 59 per cent achieve this level. Even more worryingly, by the age of 19 they are more than twice as likely as other students not to be in education, work or training and girls are much more likely to become pregnant very young. Statistically, it cannot be the case that this group of students are so much less able than others, which suggests that there must be massive underachievement. Undoubtedly, some of these students must be gifted or talented. (BBC 2007)

Lack of educational resources is a major hurdle that many looked after children have to overcome. Without sustained parental support, they rarely get places at the best schools. Foster carers are, understandably, often more concerned with feeding, clothing and dealing with emotional and behavioural problems than with education. They may be unaware of the value of attending parents'/carers' evenings; making sure that students can go to after-school clubs; and checking that they have the right equipment and access to computers. They are less likely to offer them enrichment activities at weekends and during school holidays. Even when looked after children settle into foster homes on a long-term basis, it is difficult for outsiders to appreciate the emotional turmoil, guilt associated with rejection, and attachment difficulties that inhibit learning and relationships with other people.

It is very easy for teachers to become so preoccupied with what looked after children cannot or will not do, that they may miss the skills and abilities that they do have or could develop, given sufficient support and opportunities.

Fortunately, the integration of children's services envisaged in *Every Child Matters* and the *Care Matters: Time for Change* white paper of 2007 aims to redress this situation.

1. Local Authorities (LAs) will be expected to provide high quality early years experiences for young looked after children.
2. LAs will be expected to make sure that looked after children have priority admission to schools that are best able to meet their needs and abilities.
3. Moving looked after students in Years 10 and 11 will be considered only as a last resort.
4. Grants of £500 are to be made to any looked after children who are not likely to meet expected standards. This money could be used for individual tuition or computer equipment.
5. Free music tuition and access to other activities are to be made available so that these students have the same opportunities as others to develop their abilities.
6. Bursaries of at least £2,000 will be available for any looked after student going on to higher education.

Possibly the best way for looked after students' educational needs to be met in schools is for a Personal Education Plan (PEP) to be drawn up for each one. To be effective, the children themselves and carers will need to be fully involved in the process. Where gifts and talents are identified (and they should be actively sought), schools should make sure that:

1. All impediments to developing these abilities are tackled, whether these are problems associated with lack of confidence and low aspirations or those concerning access to out-of-school activities such as transport, lack of equipment or funding for courses.
2. Clear manageable targets, that do not overwhelm young people whose confidence has already been damaged, should be set and every small step towards those targets recognized and applauded.
3. Account is taken of crisis times, such as change of placement or the reappearance of an absent parent, when performance and attitude are likely to deteriorate.
4. Information from previous schools is used (and demanded where it is not provided) so that past performance can be built on.
5. There is continuity of support from a designated adult within the school.

Case Study

Lorna was the second of four children. Her mother was an alcoholic and day-to-day management of the home fell to Lorna and her older brother. Social workers were monitoring the family but the standard of care the children received was very low. The home was dirty and smelly and the children often went hungry.

When she was 12, Lorna ran away to escape the chaos but was found by the police and brought back. When the police saw the conditions in which the children were living, they were all taken into care.

The smaller children were adopted but Lorna and her older brother were considered too old and, in any case, wanted to maintain contact with the mother. The social workers decided, without consulting them, that Lorna and her brother should be kept together and a placement was found in the next town. This meant that Lorna had to change schools. She was desperately unhappy because she was not close to this brother but missed the smaller siblings with whom contact was denied and yearned for the company of some good friends at her previous school. As her behaviour at the new school deteriorated, a case conference was held. This time, Lorna's views were taken into account and she was moved away from her brother to another placement where she could go to her old school.

Teachers were not overjoyed to hear that Lorna would be returning because of her absenteeism and disruptive behaviour. She did, however, have a good relationship with a teacher of English, who – despite scepticism from others – maintained that Lorna was a very able student. This teacher readily agreed to act as a mentor. One of the first things she did was to arrange to meet up with the new foster mother and Lorna. Armed with information from other subject teachers, they sat down together and agreed a PEP. Initial targets were simple and straightforward like getting homework in on time. Her previous chaotic lifestyle had made this almost impossible. Her targets in English were more demanding, reflecting her ability in this field. The foster mother agreed that Lorna could attend theatre club every Wednesday and transport arrangements were made with another parent who lived nearby. The mentor also provided the foster mother with a list of books that Lorna should be reading and arranged to lend her some of her own copies. All three went to the local library and signed Lorna up. The foster mother also signed up the other small child she was fostering and arranged to take him to some of the story time sessions in the afternoons. She had not realized that these opportunities existed.

Slowly Lorna is getting there and was incredibly proud to achieve a Level 7 in English at the end of KS3. She is now on the gifted and talented register and regularly takes part in school and house productions. On her good days, she is beginning to talk about university and her mentor allowed her to join a group of Year 10 students who were visiting Oxford. There are still days when she is uncooperative and aggressive to teachers but there is a much greater understanding of Lorna within the staffroom. Lorna is becoming more self-aware and able to apologize when she is in the wrong. Unfortunately her mentor will be leaving the school soon but another young teacher has slowly been taking over her role so that Lorna does not feel abandoned. She too has established contact with the foster mother and is hoping that she can help Lorna to maintain momentum and get a place at a good university. Everyone is holding their breath.

Poor or Unsupported Students

We still have over three million children living in poverty in the UK. They may be:

- recent immigrants or refugees
- the offspring of low paid parents/carers
- the offspring of parents with mental or physical disabilities
- the offspring of the long-term unemployed
- travellers.

In every case it will be difficult for them to do justice to their abilities in school because:

1. The parents do not have the financial resources to buy books, computers and other essentials.
2. They may not have transport so that they can visit different places and get to music lessons or clubs. Children travel up to 100 miles to attend Saturday music academies in London and Manchester. The poor cannot access such resources.
3. Their parents' expectations are often low. If they did not do well at school themselves, they do not expect it to be beneficial to their children.
4. Lifestyles may be chaotic and getting to school every day and on time may seem unimportant.
5. Sadly, some parents discourage their children from engaging with school in case they do well and reject the family lifestyle.
6. Some cultures and social groups do not value learning for girls or some specific abilities, such as art, music or ballet.

For all of these children, it is important that teachers at all stages:

- believe in their ability to do well
- scrutinize standardized tests such as CATs for evidence of high ability
- pick up on curiosity about certain topics or subjects and look out for perceptive questions or answers
- work on the assumption that the vast majority of parents experience pride in the children's achievements and actively involve them in celebrating good work or performance
- enter children of high ability for the Young, Gifted and Talented programme and actively encourage them to take part in local and regional events
- work through the leading teacher for gifted and talented education to find a way of overcoming any financial or practical barriers to poor or unsupported children taking part in events
- look for role models and mentors within the school or community or in local business to nurture such children.

Isolated and Unhappy Students

Where gifted and talented students do become unhappy and isolated, this may be because of:

- labelling
- family relationships
- pressure from teachers
- personality traits that irritate their peers.

Labelling a child gifted can be a great burden. Peers may become jealous and start to 'snipe'. The gifted students themselves may feel under pressure to meet what they often regard as the unrealistic expectations of parents and teachers. Some very able students in Excellence in Cities schools asked their teachers not to identify them as gifted and opted not to take part in enrichment/extension activities. They feared they would become estranged from their friends. Whatever the reason, when a student feels threatened by the gifted or talented label, the matter will have to be handled with great sensitivity by schools and parents and the student's point of view respected.

Most parents want their children to succeed and offer whatever support they can to help them but a few unwittingly play out their own ambitions vicariously through their children. They convince themselves that when they exert pressure to succeed, it is for the children's good. They are equally convinced that their children do not really mean it when they say that they do not want to be a doctor or a mathematician or a tennis star. *Gifted* by Nikita Lalwani is an excellent fictional example of how parental pressure can make children isolated and unhappy.

Freeman (1998) cites a piece of research from China where 115 children with extremely high IQs were hot-housed by parents and teachers. Academically they were outstanding but they were found to be 'lacking in easy social relationships, and the parents had to be given some more lessons in how to help their children to have some social life'. (1998:28)

Schools can help such students by:

- trying to get them involved in social activities with other students
- setting up a befriending scheme so that older pupils or even people from outside the school meet up and talk with them; sometimes it can be useful to find someone who shares their interests
- involving them in non-academic activities
- making it clear to the students that they are valued for themselves
- using counsellors or mentors to listen and advise; underachieving but very able girls at a selective school enthused about the counsellor who met up with them on a regular basis to talk about their progress and their problems – it was important that she was not a member of the school and they felt able to talk without hurting anyone's feelings (Goodhew 2004)
- working with parents to help them understand the importance of social interaction with others and time 'to be'.

There are times when it is teachers who apply the pressure. At primary level league tables can be the catalyst. Later, subject specialists press their own interests unaware that every other subject teacher is doing the same thing to the same children, as in the following case study.

Case Study

Simon, Year 11, was every teacher's dream – a very hard-working high achiever. He had already gained his silver Duke of Edinburgh Award, was a flute player in the school and area youth orchestra, potential head boy, charming and cooperative. He was taking 12 GCSEs and every teacher expected him to get an A*. When he also found girls he became less focused and teachers became anxious. Entreaties came from all directions to give priority to particular projects or assignments. The PE teacher wanted him to join the rugby team, the head of music wanted to involve him in an evening concert and his head of house wanted him to organize the house sports event. Simon began to feel that he was carrying everyone's expectations and considered dropping out. On the advice of a sympathetic teacher, he spoke to the headteacher who instructed all teachers to give him space. They did – reluctantly – but he decided his own priorities and plucked up the courage to turn down the offer of the rugby team and the chance to organize the house sports event.

Some gifted and talented students apply ridiculous levels of pressure to themselves. The perfectionists cannot accept anything other than the best and may take ages to complete every task. These young people will spend ages on homework at primary level and will often sit up into the small hours as they get older, fearful of making mistakes and not living up to their self-imposed standards. Parents and teachers should be on the lookout for these able students. They may need counselling, reassurance and determination on the part of teachers and parents to draw them away from their academic work occasionally so that they get a more balanced perspective.

Perhaps one of the most difficult groups of gifted and talented students to deal with are those who are excessively goal-orientated and competitive. Whatever they do, getting there first is more important than admiring the view on the way. Sometimes there is barely concealed contempt for those who progress at a more sedentary pace and a lack of awareness of how their manner offends others. Such students can become very isolated unless measures are taken to modify their outlook. Unfortunately a few parents exacerbate the situation by encouraging their children's negative attitudes to their peers and a blinkered and narrow approach to learning. A sensitive home/school liaison programme together with academic and social mentoring from someone the student both likes and respects may help. It could also be helpful to set targets for working as part of a team and to adopt a problem-solving approach that requires careful thought and research rather than a first-past-the-post approach.

Black and Minority Ethnicity (BME) and English as an Additional Language (EAL)

Black and Minority Ethnicity

The under-representation of some BME students on gifted and talented registers and programmes, especially in secondary schools, is well recorded, although it needs to be said that some groups, such as Chinese, Indian and Irish may also be over-represented. Where Black students do appear to be reasonably well represented on a gifted and talented register, closer scrutiny often reveals that they are there for sporting ability but rarely for academic ability. The groups that cause most concern are Black Africans, Afro-Caribbeans and Muslims of Bangladeshi, Pakistani or Somali origin.

In a paper written for the Open Society Institute (2005) it was suggested that schools need to think more about religious diversity rather than ethnicity. It attributes the underperformance of Muslims in UK schools to:

- religious prejudice and Islamophobia
- lack of Muslim role models in school
- low level parental involvement in schools
- low teacher expectation of these pupils
- a European and Christian basis to the curriculum with little reference to the part played by the Muslim world in the field of art, mathematics, geometry, science, philosophy, astronomy and medicine
- lack of awareness of teachers and pupils to Muslim sensitivity about modesty, which can impact on performance in PE, sport, drama and art
- lack of awareness amongst Christians of the attitudes of some Muslim groups to music; in some cases it is simply not valued and in others it is considered undesirable.

Given that Black and Muslim students often do very well in academic subjects at KS1 and KS2, their poor performance at secondary level cannot easily be attributed to lack of ability.

For some Black boys, being treated in a way that they consider disrespectful or likely to cause them loss of face can also contribute to their underachievement, as can a curriculum that appears to have no relevance to their lives and experiences. For both Black and Muslim students, their gifts and talents are likely to go unnoticed until:

1. Stereotyping is avoided so that teachers have the same high academic expectations for these students as they do for White students and encourage them to raise their aspirations.

   A good case study of how this can be done with girls, mainly from the Muslim community, can be found at Teachernet (2007). Three London state secondary schools, including Mulberry School for Girls, joined forces with the independent City of London School for Girls and organized eight five-hour Saturday workshops, concentrating on critical thinking skills and academic subjects. Thirty able, but in some cases underachieving, girls from the three state schools were involved. The teaching was carried out by five teachers from the independent school with the help of teachers from the state schools. Parents were invited to the final sessions. As a result of these workshops, students' performance and confidence in core subjects were raised. Disaffected and underachieving girls particularly benefited from the extra attention and recognition of their potential.

Ten London schools have managed to raise the performance of Somali students to such an extent that in one secondary school, 100 per cent achieved five or more A*–C and in a primary schools 94 per cent achieved Level 4 or above even though English was not their first language. Researchers found that the factors contributing to this success were:

- 'strong, inspirational leadership by headteacher and management team
- close links with parents and increasing community support
- effective use of diverse workforce
- effective support for pupils for whom English is not a first language and a broad curriculum which incorporates aspects of pupils' own culture adding relevance and building self-esteem
- successful recruitment of staff reflecting the local community
- Somali learning mentors making successful links with the local community, parents and pupils.' (NALDIC 2008)

2. Serious efforts are made to adapt the curriculum so that their cultures and experiences are seen to be valued and relevant. Alderman (2008:35) shows how science units at KS3 were tweaked to make them more relevant to African and Caribbean students. Three examples are included in the following table:

Modifying Science Units at KS3 to Make Them More Relevant to African and Caribbean students		
Unit	Title	Examples
7A	Cells	Compare red blood cells with sickle cells. Comparison of pollen grains across continents to map continental drift.
8D	Ecological Relationships	African and Caribbean animals and plants.
9D	Plants and Food Production	Global food production, vegetables imported from African countries.

3. Much greater efforts are made by schools to involve parents and to recruit an ethnically and culturally diverse workforce and to use mentors from the local community. Instead of expecting parents to come in to schools, it may be necessary for schools to identify where they do gather (e.g. churches, community centres, health centres) and to make contact in places where they are comfortable.

English as an Additional Language (EAL) Students

The problems experienced by some EAL students in accessing the curriculum and the difficulties teachers have in assessing their true ability are very understandable. Sometimes they are made worse because we misread the signals these students give.

1. Some students avoid eye contact as a mark of respect, not because they do not want to engage with the lesson. This can be very confusing for a British, Australian or US teacher where eye contact is considered very important.
2. Similarly, students who nod and smile vigorously do not necessarily understand what is going on but they may wish to please the teacher and avoid losing face.
3. Students who refuse to speak may be embarrassed by their poor command of the language. It does not mean that they lack interest or ability.
4. EAL students may not produce a great deal of work if they are struggling to get to grips with the lesson. Again it may not indicate lack of ability or interest.

EAL students can be helped to reveal their true ability by:

1. Using a range of strategies, that do not demand a good understanding of English, to assess their potential. This might include NVR tests, Raven's Coloured Progressive Matrices, checklists of behaviours. Some subject-specific tests can be translated into their own language. If first language assessments are available they should be used.
2. Teaching the language required to understand different subjects, not just key subject words but what were referred to in Chapter 5 as 'head words', the words needed to understand the tasks. One school in Leicester holds an English for maths class after school once a week for students in the early stages of acquiring English.

   'In this time the students concentrate on the language they require to understand or explain mathematical concepts rather than on maths itself. The first KS4 group to try this yielded students who had been predicted grade E at the start of year 11 actually obtaining grades B or C. The first KS3 class has seen students moved up several sets for the start of KS4.' (SFE)
3. Providing them with bilingual dictionaries and allowing them to use their mother tongue to clarify key concepts. Use ICT to give them access to translation tools and first language resources.
4. Using visuals such as graphs, pictures, diagrams, maps, etc. to illustrate key points of the lesson.
5. Giving them access to subject-specific writing frames, authoring programmes and other scaffolding devices.
6. Motivating them to use English through video conferencing, email, virtual classrooms and web page authoring and collaborative work with others.

As with Black and ethnic minority students, adapt some units of work so that they are relevant to EAL students' experiences.

Appendix 1

INSTITUTIONAL QUALITY STANDARDS IN GIFTED AND TALENTED EDUCATION

Generic Elements	Entry	Developing	Exemplary
A – Effective teaching and learning strategies			
Identification	The school/college has learning conditions and systems to identify gifted and talented pupils in all year groups and an agreed definition and shared understanding of the meaning of 'gifted and talented' within its own, local and national contexts.	Individual pupils are screened annually against clear criteria at school/college and subject/topic level.	**Multiple criteria** and **sources of evidence** are used to identify gifts and talents, including through the use of a broad range of quantitative and qualitative data.
	An **accurate record** of the identified gifted and talented population is kept and updated.	The record is used to identify underachievement and **exceptional achievement** (both within and outside the population) and to track/review pupil **progress.**	The record is supported by a comprehensive monitoring, progress planning and reporting system which all staff regularly share and contribute to.
	The identified gifted and talented population broadly reflects the school/college's **social and economic composition,** gender and ethnicity.	**Identification** systems address issues of **multiple exceptionality** (pupils with specific gifts/talents and special educational needs).	**Identification** processes are regularly reviewed and refreshed in the light of pupil performance and value-added data. The gifted and talented population is fully representative of the school/college's population.
Evidence			
Next steps			

Glossary definition provided for words and phrases shown in bold in the accompanying Quality Standard' User Guide

QS Model October 2005

Generic Elements	Entry	Developing	Exemplary
Effective provision in the classroom	The school/college addresses the different needs of the gifted and talented population by providing a stimulating learning environment and by extending the teaching repertoire.	Teaching and learning strategies are diverse and flexible, meeting the needs of distinct pupil groups within the gifted and talented population (e.g. able underachievers, exceptionally able).	The school/college has established a range of methods to find out what works best in the classroom, and shares this within the school/college and with other schools and colleges.
	Teaching and learning is differentiated and delivered through both individual and group activities.	A range of challenging learning and teaching strategies is evident in lesson planning and delivery. **Independent learning** skills are developed.	Teaching and learning are suitably challenging and varied, incorporating the **breadth, depth** and **pace** required to progress high achievement. Pupils routinely work independently and self-reliantly.
	Opportunities exist to extend learning through **new technologies.**	The use of **new technologies** across the curriculum is focused on **personalized learning** needs.	The innovative use of **new technologies** raises the achievement and motivation of gifted and talented pupils.
Evidence			
Next steps			
Standards	Levels of **attainment** and **achievement** for gifted and talented pupils are comparatively high in relation to the rest of the school/college population and are in line with those of similar pupils in similar schools/colleges.	Levels of **attainment** and **achievement** for gifted and talented pupils are broadly consistent across the gifted and talented population and above those of similar pupils in similar schools/colleges.	Levels of **attainment** and **achievement** for gifted and talented pupils indicate sustainability over time and are well above those of similar pupils in similar schools/colleges.
	Self-evaluation indicates that gifted and talented provision is satisfactory.	Self-evaluation indicates that gifted and talented provision is good.	Self-evaluation indicates that gifted and talented provision is very good or excellent.
	Schools'/colleges' gifted and talented education programmes are explicitly linked to the achievement of SMART outcomes and these highlight improvements		

	in pupils' attainment and achievement.		
Evidence			
Next steps			
B – Enabling curriculum entitlement and choice			
Enabling curriculum entitlement and choice	Curriculum organization is flexible, with opportunities for enrichment and increasing subject/topic choice. Pupils are provided with support and guidance in making choices.	The curriculum offers opportunities and guidance to pupils which enable them to work beyond their age and/or phase, and across subjects or topics, according to their aptitudes and interests.	The curriculum offers **personalized learning pathways** for pupils which maximize individual **potential**, retain flexibility of future choices, extend well beyond test/examination requirements and result in sustained impact on pupil **attainment and achievement.**
Evidence			
Next steps			
C – Assessment for learning			
Assessment for learning	Processes of data analysis and pupil assessment are employed throughout the school/college to plan learning for gifted and talented pupils.	Routine progress reviews, using both qualitative and quantitative data, make effective use of prior, predictive and value-added **attainment** data to plan for progression in pupils' learning.	**Assessment data** are used by teachers and across the school/college to ensure challenge and sustained progression in individual pupils' learning.
	Dialogue with pupils provides focused feedback which is used to plan future learning.	Systematic oral and written feedback helps pupils to set challenging curricular targets.	Formative assessment and individual target setting combine to maximize and celebrate pupils' achievements.
	Self- and peer-assessment, based on clear understanding of criteria, are used to increase pupils' responsibility for learning.	Pupils reflect on their own skill development and are involved in the design of their own targets and tasks.	Classroom practice regularly requires pupils to reflect on their own **progress** against targets, and engage in the direction of their own learning.
Evidence			
Next steps			

Glossary definition provided for words and phases shown in bold in the accompanying Quality Standard' User Guide

QS Model October 2005

Generic Elements	Entry	Developing	Exemplary
D – School/college organization			
School/college ethos and pastoral care	The school/college sets high expectations, recognizes achievement and celebrates the successes of all its pupils.	The school/college fosters an environment which promotes positive behaviour for learning. Pupils are listened to and their views taken into account.	An ethos of ambition and achievement is agreed and shared by the whole school/college community. Success across a wide range of abilities is celebrated.
	The school/college identifies and addresses the particular social and emotional needs of gifted and talented pupils in consultation with pupils, parents and carers.	Strategies exist to counteract bullying and any adverse effects of social and curriculum pressures. Specific support for able underachievers and pupils from different cultures and social backgrounds is available and accessible.	The school/college places equal emphasis on high achievement and emotional well-being, underpinned by programmes of support, personalized to the needs of gifted and talented pupils. There are opportunities for pupils to use their gifts to benefit other pupils and the wider community.
Evidence			
Next Steps			
Transfer and transition	Shared processes, using agreed criteria, are in place to ensure the productive transfer of information from one setting to another (i.e. from class to class, year to year and school/college to school/college).	Transfer information concerning gifted and talented pupils, including parental input, informs targets for pupils to ensure **progress** in learning. Particular attention is given to including new admissions.	Transfer data concerning gifted and talented pupils are used to inform planning of teaching and learning at subject/aspect/topic and individual pupil level, and to ensure progression according to ability rather than age or phase.
Evidence			
Next steps			
Leadership	A named member of the governing body, senior management team and the lead professional responsible for gifted and talented education have clearly directed responsibilities for motivating and driving gifted and talented provision. The	**Responsibility** for gifted and talented provision is **distributed,** and evaluation of its impact shared, at all levels in the school/ college. Staff subscribe to policy at all levels. Governors play a significant supportive and evaluative role.	Organizational structures, communication channels and the deployment of staff (e.g. workforce remodelling) are flexible and creative in supporting the delivery of **personalized learning.** Governors take a lead in

	(Entry)	(Developing)	(Exemplary)
	headteacher actively champions gifted and talented provision.		celebrating achievements of gifted and talented pupils.
Evidence			
Next steps			
Policy	The gifted and talented policy is integral to the school/college's inclusion agenda and approach to personalized learning, feeds into and from the single school/college improvement plan and is consistent with other policies.	The policy directs and reflects best practice in the school/college, is regularly reviewed and is clearly linked to other policy documentation.	The policy includes input from the whole school/college community and is regularly refreshed in the light of innovative national and international practice.
	Pupils participate in dedicated gifted and talented activities (e.g. summer schools) and their participation is recorded.	Local and national provision helps meet individual pupils' learning needs e.g. NAGTY membership, accessing outreach local enrichment programmes.	Coherent strategies are used to direct and develop individual expert performance via external agencies e.g. HE/FE links, online support, and local/regional/national programmes.
Evidence			
Next steps			
Monitoring and evaluation	**Subject and phase audits** focus on the quality of teaching and learning for gifted and talented pupils. Whole school/college targets are set using prior **attainment** data.	Performance against targets (including at pupil level) is regularly reviewed. Targets include qualitative pastoral and curriculum outcomes as well as numerical data.	Performance against targets is rigorously evaluated against clear criteria. Qualitative and quantitative outcomes inform whole school/college self-evaluation processes.
	Elements of provision are planned against clear objectives within effective whole-school self-evaluation processes.	All elements, including non-academic aspects of gifted and talented provision, are planned to clear objectives and are subjected to detailed evaluation.	The school/college examines and challenges its own provision to inform development of further experimental and innovative practice in collaboration with other schools/colleges.
Evidence			
Next steps			

Glossary definition provided for words and phases shown in bold in the accompanying Quality Standard' User Guide

QS Model October 2005

Generic Elements	Entry	Developing	Exemplary
Strong partnerships beyond the school			
Engaging with the community, families and beyond	Parents/carers are aware of the school's/college's policy on gifted and talented provision, contribute to its **identification** processes and are kept informed of developments in gifted and talented provision, including through the School Profile.	Progression of gifted and talented pupils is enhanced by home-school/college partnerships. There are strategies to engage and support hard-to-reach parents/carers.	Parents/carers are actively engaged in extending provision. Support for gifted and talented provision is integrated with other children's services (e.g. Sure Start, EAL, traveller, refugee, **LAC** Services).
	The school/college shares good practice and has some collaborative provision with other schools, colleges and the wider community.	A coherent strategy for networking with other schools, colleges and local community organizations extends and enriches provision.	There is strong emphasis on collaborative and innovative working with other schools/colleges which impacts on quality of provision locally, regionally and nationally.
Evidence			
Next steps			
Learning beyond the classroom	There are opportunities for pupils to learn beyond the school/college day and site (extended hours and out-of-school activities).	A coherent programme of enrichment and extension activities (through extended hours and out of school activities) complements teaching and learning and helps identify pupils' latent gifts and talents.	Innovative models of learning beyond the classroom are developed in collaboration with local and national schools/colleges to further enhance teaching and learning.
	Pupils participate in dedicated gifted and talented activities (e.g. summer schools) and their participation is recorded.	Local and national provision helps meet individual pupils' learning needs e.g. NAGTY membership, accessing outreach, local enrichment programmes.	Coherent strategies are used to direct and develop individual expert performance via external agencies e.g. HE/FE links, online support, and local/regional/national programmes.
Evidence			
Next steps			
Staff development	Staff have received professional development in meeting the needs of gifted and talented pupils.	The induction programme for new staff addresses gifted and talented issues, both at whole-school/	There is ongoing audit of staff needs and an appropriate range of professional development in gifted

	college and specific subject/aspect level.		and talented education. Professional development is informed by research and collaboration within and beyond the school/college.
	The lead professional responsible for gifted and talented education has received appropriate professional development.	Subject/aspect and phase leaders have received specific professional development in meeting the needs of gifted and talented pupils.	Priorities for the development of gifted and talented provision are included within a professional development entitlement for all staff and are monitored through performance management processes.
Evidence			
Next Steps			
Resources	Provision for gifted and talented pupils is supported by appropriate budgets and resources.	Allocated resources include school/college-based and nationally available resources, and these have a significant and measurable impact on the progress that pupils make and their attitudes to learning.	Resources are used to stimulate innovative and experimental practice, which is shared throughout the school/college and regularly reviewed for impact and best value.
Evidence			
Next steps			

Glossary definition provided for words and phrases shown in bold in the accompanying Quality Standard' User Guide

QS Model October 2005

Appendix 2

Acceleration Checklist

Before accelerating a child, have you:	Yes/No
1. Explored all available strategies for providing for that child within his/her peer group?	

2. Consulted fully with:
    Parents *(Such consultation should include advice on pros and cons of acceleration and time for parents to consider this information.)*
    Teachers
    The child *(Children are rarely consulted or involved in the process)*
    Any receiving schools or colleges *(Are they prepared to accept young pupils? Can they provide appropriate programmes of study for them?)*	

3. Considered:
    The emotional/social maturity of the child?
    The physical maturity of the child?
    Areas of weakness within curriculum *(e.g. presentation skills or spelling)*?
    The friendship ties of the child?
    The long-term impact on the child?
(e.g. There can be conflict at adolescence between parents and children when children want to socialize with and behave like their classmates and not their chronological age group. Is the child likely to benefit from going to university early?)	

4. Drawn up a short-term plan with all concerned parties for the pupil's educational provision?	
5. Made arrangements for regular review of the pupil's progress throughout his/her schooling?	
6. Told parents, child and teachers of agencies that can support them if there are difficulties? *(E.g. NAGC or CHI.)*	

Appendix 3

Opportunities and Support for Gifted and Talented Students

General		
Young, Gifted and Talented	www.ygt.dcsf.gov.uk	News of national and local courses. Resources for students, teachers and parents. Portal to other organizations.

E-Learning and Mentoring		
Astronomy.ac.uk	www.astronomy.ac.uk	Opportunities to study astronomy at Cert HE level. Usually open to those who have finished secondary schooling but exceptions have been made.
British Council	http://www.britishcouncil.org/	Opportunities for travel abroad and exchanges for older students.
Cambridge School Classics Project	http://www.cambridgescp.com	Opportunities to learn Latin where schools cannot provide it.
Faulkes Telescope	http://faulkestelescope.com/education/gifted_talented	KS3 upwards with special section on gifted and talented use of this facility.
NRICH	www.nrich.maths.org	Maths activities for all key stages
World Class Tests	www.worldclassarena.org.uk	Maths and problem-solving tests for very able students and some online maths resources.
Young Applicants in School and Colleges Scheme (YASS) – Open University	http://www.open.ac.uk/yass/	Undergraduate modules for exceptionally able Year 12/13 students.

Activities and Courses		
Arvon Foundation	www.arvonfoundation.org	Residential creative writing courses led by professional writers.
Being Heard	www.beingheard.org.uk	Website for young people interested in politics.

British Schools Exploring Society	http://www.bses.org.uk/index.php	Summer expeditions for 16–20-year-olds.
Cambridge Schools Classics Project	www.cambridgescp.com	Opportunities to learn Latin independently or with teacher facilitator.
Debating Academy	http://www.britishdebate.co.uk/schools/	Residential debating course for 14+.
Headstart Engineering	http://www.headstartcourses.org.uk/	High quality courses for 16+.
Hoagies' Gifted Education	http://www.hoagiesgifted.org/index.htm	Activities and information for gifted students and their parents.
Institute of Physics	www.iop.org	Details of a range of science and engineering activities for age 9 upwards can be found here.
Plus	http://plus.maths.org/index.html	Online maths magazine for older mathematicians.
Rockwatch	www.rockwatch.org.uk	Junior branch of Geological Association. Branches throughout country.
Royal Society of Chemistry	http://www.chemsoc.org	Activities mainly for KS3 upwards but the Bill Bryson Science Communication Award is open to primary schools. Runs Salters Chemistry Camps with other organizations.
Smallpiece Engineering	http://www.smallpeicetrust.org.uk/	Residential engineering courses for 12–18s.
Space School UK	http://www.spaceschooluk.org/	Residential space course for 13+.
UK Youth Parliament	www.ukyouthparliament.org.uk	Secondary schools throughout UK eligible to take part in this annual event.
Villiers Park	www.villierspark.org.uk	Advanced residential courses for Year 12/13 students.
WISE	www.wisecampaign.org.uk	Information and courses for girls wishing to enter engineering.
Young Archaeologists Clubs	www.britarch.ac.uk/yac	Network of clubs for primary and secondary throughout country.
Young Enterprise	www.young-enterprise.org.uk	15-19-year-olds. Have to set up company and run it for a year.
Youth Dance England	www.yde.org.uk	Database of dance opportunities all over the country.

Competitions and Awards		
BA Science Communicator Awards	www.the-ba.net	Awards at three levels for 11–16-year-olds to encourage communication of scientific ideas.
Crest Awards	www.the-ba.net	Science awards for 11–19-year-olds
English Speaking Union	www.esu.org	Debates and public speaking competitions – secondary.
Eurotalk Junior Language Challenge	http://eurotalk.com/jlc/	Primary. Annual competition which exposes students to a number of different languages.
Film Education	http://www.filmeducation.org/	Occasional awards for film criticism and scriptwriting and other aspects of film making for primary and secondary students.
First Light Movies	http://firstlight.3forming.com	Funds and inspires film making with 5–18-year-olds.
Foyle Young Poet of the Year Award	www.poetrysociety.org.uk/content/competitions/fyp/	Annual award for 11–17-year-olds.
Geographical Association	http://www.geography.org.uk/events/worldwise/	Geography-based quizzes for primary and secondary schools.
John Muir Awards	www.johnmuiraward.org	All ages. Awards for anyone interested in conservation.
Newsday Competition	http://www.newsday.co.uk/index.php	For all ages. Annual competition to create newspaper or news website in a day.
Robocup Junior Challenge	http://rcj.open.ac.uk	Age 8+. Design and build robots to carry out certain tasks.
The Arts Award	www.artsaward.org.uk	Secondary. An award scheme, similar in structure to the Duke of Edinburgh Award Scheme, to encourage artists and art leaders to develop their talents.
UK Chess Challenge	http://ukchesschallenge.com	National competition for all ages and abilities.
UKMT	www.mathcomp.leeds.ac.uk	Secondary maths challenges and mentoring.
Young Composer Competition	www.bbc.co.uk/proms/2008/youngcomposers/	Secondary annual award.
Young Engineers	www.youngeng.org	Lots of competitions at all levels.

Specialist Music and Dance Schools in DSCF Aided Places Scheme		
Arts Education School, Tring	www.aes-tring.com	Ages 11+. Performing Arts school.
Chethams School, Manchester	www.chethams.com	Ages 8+. Residential or day music school.
Choir Schools Scholarship Scheme	www.choirschools.org.uk	Scholarships for students from low income families to train at one of 36 choir schools throughout the country.
Elmhurst School of Dance, Birmingham	www.elmhurstdance.co.uk	Ages 11+. Specializes in ballet.
Hammond School, Chester	www.thehammondschool.co.uk	Ages 11+. Dance and drama.
Purcell School of Music, Herts	www.purcell-school.org	Ages 9+. Instrumental tuition.
Royal Ballet School, London	www.royal-ballet-school.org.uk	Ages 11+.
St Mary's Music School, Edinburgh	www.st-marys-music-school.co.uk	Ages 9+. All instruments.
Wells Cathedral School, Somerset	www.wells-cathedral-school.com	Age 8+. All instruments.
Yehudi Menuhin School, Surrey	www.yehudimenuhinschool.co.uk	Age 8+. Strings and keyboard only.
Most specialist music colleges run Saturday academies for talented young musicians.		

Support and Counselling		
CHI	http://www.chiorg.ndo.co.uk	Advocacy for exceptionally able students.
NAGC	www.nagcbritain.org.uk/	Activities, courses and support for gifted and talented students and their families.

Appendix 4

Essential Online Resources for Teachers

Organization	Contact details	Support provided
Becta	www.becta.org.uk	Advice on using ICT in the classroom.
G&T Update	www.teachingexpertise.com	Magazine providing up to date info on gifted and talented education.
Hoagies	www.hoagiesgifted.org	Gifted and talented resources.
NACE	www.nace.co.uk	Resources & training for teachers. Day a Week School. Challenge Award.
NAGC	www.nagcbritain.org.uk/	Support and activities for gifted and talented children and their families.
NRICH	www.nrich.maths.org	Maths resources for children, teachers and parents.
Primary National Strategies	http://www.standards.dfes.gov.uk/primary/	Guidance for teachers. Several publications.
QCA	www.qca.org.uk	Subject specific guidance on teaching gifted and talented students. AfL guidance.
Secondary National Strategies	http://www.standards.dfes.gov.uk/secondary	Guidance for teachers. Several publications
Stemnet	http://www.stemnet.org.uk	Regional Setpoints provide schools with access to experts and activities in science, maths, engineering and technology.
World Council for Gifted and Talented Children	www.world-gifted.org	World-wide advocacy for gifted children.
World Wide Arena	www.worldclassarena.org	Maths tests and support material for top 10 per cent of ability range.
YG&T	www.ygt.dcsf.gov.uk	Portal for teachers, students and parents seeking resources, courses, training. Links to regional hubs and regional gifted and talented partnerships.

Bibliography

Ainsworth, P. (2007), 'Pupils respond to a teacher's marking'. *G&T Update*, 46, 8.

Alderman, T. (2008), *Meeting the Needs of Your Most Able Pupils: Science*. London: Routledge.

Barnes, S. (2007), *Meeting the Needs of Your Most Able Pupils: History*. London: Routledge.

Bauby, J.-D. (2008), *The Diving Bell and the Butterfly*. London: Harper Perennial.

BBC (2007), *Schools to help children in care*. [Online]. Available at http://news.bbc.co.uk/1/hi/education/6221778.stm. [Accessed 1 May 2008]

Braggett, E. (1997), *Differentiated Programs for Primary Schools: Units of Work for Gifted and Talented Students*. Cheltenham, Victoria: Hawker Brownlow Education.

Brown, G. and Wragg, E. (1993), *Questioning*. London: Routledge.

Chi-Charity (2005), *The Support Society for Children of High Intelligence*. [Online]. (Updated 29 October 2007) Available at http://www.chi-charity.org.uk. [Accessed 9 March 2008]

Clark, C. (1995), 'Teaching thinking skills to able learners'. *Flying High*, 2, 6–8.

Clark, C. and Callow, R. (1998), *Educating Able Children*. London: David Fulton Publishers.

Darley, H. and McGoldrick, A. (2005), *Bridging the gap: bigging up boys' writing*. [Online]. Available at http://ygt.dcsf.gov.uk/FileLinks/362_helen_darley_and_april_mcgoldrick.pdf. [Accessed 26 March 2008]

De Bono, E. (2000), *Six Thinking Hats*. London: Penguin Books.

De Bono, E. *CORT Thinking Program* CD. Oxford: Cavendish Information Products.

dcsf (1997–2008), *Assessment for learning – Whole-school and subject specific training materials.* [Online]. Available at http://www.standards.dfes.gov.uk/secondary/keystage3/all/respub/afl_ws. [Accessed 30 April 2008]

dcsf (2004), *Every child matters: education, training, employment.* [Online]. Available at www.everychildmatters.gov.uk/ete. [Accessed 25 April 2008]

dcsf (2005), *National quality standards.* [Online] Available at http://ygt.dcsf.gov.uk/FileLinks/347_MainLink.pdf. [Accessed 28 March 2008]

dcsf (2007), *Getting There – Able Pupils who Lose Momentum in English and Mathematics at Key Stage 2; Making Good Progress Series.* London: dcsf.

dcsf (2007), *Social and emotional aspects of learning...improving behaviour... improving learning.* [Online]. Available at http://www.standards.dcsf.gov.uk/primary/publications/banda/seal/. [Accessed 9 March 2008]

dcsf (2008), *The National Strategies – Gifted and Talented Education Guidance on Preventing Underachievement: a Focus on Exceptionally Able Pupils.* Crown copyright.

DfES dcsf (2007). *Primary and Secondary National Strategies – Gifted and Talented Education – Leading Teachers: course file and handbook.* London: DfES.

Dunn, M. D., Dunn, L. M., Whetton, C. and Burley, J. (1997), *British Picture Vocabulary Scale: Second Edition.* London: GL Assessment.

Ellison, D. (2007). *Mobilising Creativity.* [Online]. Available at http://www.schoolsnetwork.org.uk/Article.aspa?PageId=236508&NodeId=232. [Accessed 22 March 2008]

Evans, L. and Goodhew, G. (1997), *Providing for Able Children: Activities for Staff in Primary and Secondary Schools.* Dunstable: Folens Publishers.

Everything (2000), *The best teacher I ever had.* [Online]. Available at http://everything2.com/e2node/The%2520best%2520teacher%2520I%2520ever%2520had. [Accessed 28 April 2008]

Eyre, D. (1997), *Able Children in Ordinary Schools.* London: David Fulton Publishers.

Eyre, D. (2004), 'The English model of gifted and talented education'. Paper presented at the European Conference of High Ability, Pamplona.

Eyre, D. and McClure, L. (eds) (2001), *Curriculum Provision for the Gifted and Talented in the Primary School.* London: NACE/Fulton Publications.

Ferretti, J. (2007), *Meeting the Needs of Your Most Able Pupils: Geography.* London: Routledge.

Freeman, J. (1998), *Educating the Very Able: Current International Research*. London: The Stationery Office.

Freeman, J. (2001), *Gifted Children Grown Up*. London: David Fulton Publishers.

Gardner, H. (1993), *Frames of Mind*. London: Fontana Press.

Goodhew, G. (2001), 'Homework – getting it right'. *Special Children*, 142, 16–17.

Goodhew, G. (2004), *Schools Facing Challenging Circumstances – Gifted and Talented Pilot Evaluation*. London: DfES School Improvement and Excellence Division.

Griffin, N. S., Curtiss, J., McKenzie, J. and Crawford, M. (1995), 'Authentic assessment of able children using a regular classroom protocol'. *Flying High*, 2, 34–42

GT-Cyberspace (2007), *Gifted Education Policies for North Dakota*. [Online]. Available at http://www.gt-cybersource.org/StatePolicyDetails.aspx?StateCode=10029&NavID=4_0. [Accessed 7 March 2008]

Haddon, M. (2004), *The Curious Incident of the Dog in the Night-Time*. London: Vintage.

Holder, M. (2007), *Innovative graphics with maths and textile design*. [Online]. Available at http://www.schoolsnetwork.org.uk/Article.aspa?PageId=219422. [Accessed 9 April 2008]

Hunt, D. (2007), *Meeting the Needs of Your Most Able Pupils: RE*. London: Routledge.

Joseph Rowntree Foundation (2001), *Commonly-held beliefs about self-esteem are myths, warns new research review*. [Online]. Available at http://www.jrf.org.uk/pressroom/releases/281101.asp. [Accessed 19 January 2008]

Joseph Rowntree Foundation (2001), *The costs and causes of low self-esteem*. [Online]. Available at www.jrf.org.uk/knowledge/findings/socialpolicy/N71.asp. [Accessed 14 April 2008]

Keele University Research Institute for Public Policy and Management (2005), *The pupil survey*. [Online]. Available at www.keele.ac.uk/cfss/types.html. [Accessed 30 March 2008]

Lampl, P. (2007), *A Sickening Waste of Talent*. [Online]. Available at www.times online.co.uk/tol/comment/comumnists/guest_contributors/article2558. [Accessed 10 December 2007]

Leat, D. (1998), *Thinking Through Geography*. Cambridge: Chris Kington Publishing.

Lohman, D. F., Hagen, E. P. and Thorndike, R. L. (2003), *Cognitive Abilities Test: Third Edition*. London: GL Assessment.

London Gifted and Talented (2008), *REAL*. [Online]. Available at http://212.188.130.139/real/welcome. [Accessed 1 May 2008]

Montgomery, D. (2000), *Able Underachievers*. London: Whirr Publishers.

Montgomery, D. (2003), *Gifted and Talented Children with Special Educational Needs*. London: NACE/Fulton Publications.

Morley, D. and Bailey, R. (2006), *Meeting the Needs of Your Most Able Pupils: Physical Education and Sport*. London: Routledge Education.

NACE (2006), *DaWS – Day a Week School*. [Online]. Available at http://www.nace.co.uk/nace/dws/nace_daws_day_a_week_school.htm. [Accessed 14 April 2008]

NACE (2007), *Early Years Able Learners: Identification and Provision*. [Online] Available at http://www.nace.co.uk.

NAGC – The National Association for Gifted Children (2008), *NAGC Supporting all our brightest children and their families*. [Online]. Available at http://www.nagcbritain.org.uk. [Accessed 9 March 2008]

NALDIC (2008), *Somali achievement – research highlights good practice for schools*. [Online]. Available at www.naldic.org.uk/docs/news/archive/news_item.cfm?NewsID=263&Pp=1. [Accessed 19 April 2008]

Nash, P. (2005), *Raising confidence and aspirations*. [Online]. Available at www.teachernet.gov.uk/CaseStudies/casestudy.cfm?id=465. [Accessed 19 April 2008]

Neihart, M. (2000), 'Gifted children with Asperger's Syndrome'. *Gifted Child Quarterly*, 44, (4).

Open Society Institute (2005), *British Muslims and education*. [Online]. Available at www.fairuk.org/docs/OSI2004%207_Education.pdf. [Accessed 19 April 2008]

Prensky, M. (2001), *Digital natives, digital immigrants*. [Online]. Available at http://www.marcprensky.com/writing. [Accessed 20 March 2008]

QCA (1998), *Can Do Better: Raising Boys' Achievement in English*. London: QCA.

QCA (2007), *Examples of units of work: ICT – key stage 1 and 2*. [Online]. Available at http://www.qca.org.uk/qca_2228.aspx. [Accessed 21 August 2008]

Raven, J. (1983), *Coloured Progressive Matrices*. Oxford: Psychological Corporation.

Renzulli, J. S. (1998), *The three-ringed conception of giftedness*. [Online]. Available at http://www.gifted.uconn.edu/sem/semart13.html. [Accessed 6 March 2008]

Sapere (2008). *What is P4C?* [Online]. Available at http://sapere.org.uk/what-is-p4c/. [Accessed 30 April 2008]

School Doctor (2008), *Poor Handwriting – Dysgraphia*. [Online]. Available at www.schooldoctor.co.uk/13.html. [Accessed 14 April 2008]

Seltzer, K. and Bentley, T. (1999), *The Creative Age: Knowledge and Skills for the New Economy*. London: Demos.

SFE. *EAL Resource File Example*. [Online]. Available at http://www.sfe.co.uk/products/examples/EAL_examples.pdf. [Accessed 10 April 2008]

Silverman, L. K. (1989), 'Invisible gifts, invisible handicaps', *Roeper Review*, 22 (1).

Simplypsychology (2008), *Vygotsky's theory of social development*. [Online]. Available at http://simplypsychology.pwp.blueyonder.co.uk/vygotsky.html. [Accessed 2 April 2008]

South Camden City Learning Centre (2007), KS3 and KS4 gifted and talented. [Online]. Available at http://www.southcamden-clc.org.uk/KS3_&_KS4_Gifted_&_Talented.asp. [Accessed 21 August 2008]

Sports Youth Trust (2008), *Inclusion website*. [Online]. Available at http://inclusion.youthsporttrust.org/subpage/gifted-intro/index.html. [Accessed 19 April 2008]

Susskind, E. (1969), 'The role of question asking in the elementary classroom' in Kaplan, F. and Sarason, S. (eds) *The Psycho-educational Clinic*, New Haven: Yale.

The Sutton Trust (2007), *Recent Changes in Intergenerational Mobility in Britain*. [Online]. Available at http://www.suttontrust.com/reports/mainreport.pdf. [Accessed 8 March 2008]

Teachernet (2007), *Independent/state school partnerships: building bridges*. [Online]. (Updated 6 December 2007) Available at www.teachernet.gov.uk/wholeschool/buildingbridges. [Accessed 30 March 2008]

Tarr, R. (2003), *Debates and Hotseating in the History Classroom, Practical tips and advice*. [Online]. Available at http://www.schoolhistory.co.uk/forum/index.php?showtopic=2415. [Accessed 30 April 2008]

Torrance, E. P. (1980), 'Assessing the further reaches of creative potential'. *Journal of Creative Behaviour*, 14.

Training and Development Agency for Schools (2005), *Case study bigfoot theatre company*. [Online]. Available at http://www.tda.gov.uk/case_studies/remodelling/bigfoot.aspx?keywords=bigfoot. [Accessed 28 April 2008]

Training and Development Agency for Schools (2005), *Case Study: St Peter's*.

[Online]. Available at http://www.tda.gov.uk/remodelling/nationalagreement/ resources/casestudies/remodelling/st_peters.aspx. [Accessed 28 April 2008]

Urban, K. and Jellen, H. R. (1996), *Test for Creative Thinking-Drawing Production (TCT-DP)*. Oxford: Pearson Education.

Vernon, M. and La Falce-Landers, E. (1993), 'A longitudinal study of intellectually gifted deaf and hard of hearing people'. *American Annals of the Deaf*, 138 (5) 427–34.

Wallace, B. (1992), *Teaching the Very Able Child*. East Grinstead: Ward Lock Educational.

Ward, L. (2005), 'Working class children fall foul of digital divide'. *The Guardian*, [Online]. Available at http://www.guardian.co.uk/technology/2005/apr/28/ socialexclusion.elearning. [Accessed 10 January 2008]

Wells, G. (1987), *The Meaning Makers*. London: Hodder & Stoughton.

Whitmore, J.R. (1980). *Gifted, Conflict and Underachievement*. Boston: Allyn & Bacon.

Winner, E. (1996), *Gifted Children*. New York: Basic Books.

Young, Gifted and Talented (2007), The national programme for gifted and talented education. [Online]. Available at https://ygt.dcsf.gov.uk/landing.aspx. [Accessed 30 March 2008]

Index